THIS UNION CAUSE

Other books by Katherine B. Shippen

LEIF ERIKSSON

MIRACLE IN MOTION: The Story of America's Industry

PASSAGE TO AMERICA: The Story of the Great Migrations

THE POOL OF KNOWLEDGE: How the United Nations
Share Their Skills

THIS UNION CAUSE

The Growth of Organized Labor in America

by KATHERINE B. SHIPPEN

ILLUSTRATED WITH PHOTOGRAPHS AND DRAWINGS

HARPER & ROW, PUBLISHERS
NEW YORK, EVANSTON, AND LONDON

Contents

Contents

"I love this union cause. I hold it more dearly than I do my family or my life. I am willing to devote to it all that I am, or have, or hope for in the world."

William H. Sylvis

THIS UNION CAUSE

I

America Searches for Workingmen

"When you send again," Captain John Smith of the Virginia Colony wrote home to England, "I entreat you rather send but thirty carpenters, husband-men, gardeners, fishermen, masons, and diggers of trees' roots, well provided, than a thousand such as we have."

Adventurers, soldiers, and gentlemen had come to Virginia on the first three expeditions to the new country. Starvation and defeat had followed because they were incapable of the work that was necessary to clear and settle a wilderness. The Plymouth Colony had fared a little better than the Virginia one for there were craftsmen and laborers among the settlers there. That was true also in the other colonies along the eastern sea-coast. But in all of them there was need of workingmen, to cut down the big trees, to build the houses and the forts, to make the fishing boats, and clear and plant the fields.

Workingmen were the great need in all the colonies of the New World. The pressing question was how to get enough of them. At first common laborers and "diggers of trees' roots" were most needed. Then, as the country became more settled, craftsmen of every kind were in demand. The New World needed carpenters and masons, weavers and shoemakers, blacksmiths and potters.

Quite early in the country's history shiploads of Negro slaves were brought to the American ports. The first of these landed in Virginia in 1619, but others followed in New York, Boston, Philadelphia, and Baltimore. The Negroes that the slave ships brought knew nothing about the kind of work the colonists needed. They had been reared in a primitive society where the arts and crafts of Europe had never been heard of. They could do menial tasks under direction but they did not prove very useful in America until after the cotton gin had been invented and great cotton plantations had been started.

What the colonies needed was skilled man power: they needed men who understood the ways of their own people. Across the ocean in England and on the continent there were plenty of these men who were eager to try the life of the New World. In Europe there were a great many men who were able and willing to work, but there was not enough for them to do. Europe was overpopulated then. Writers of the time believed that the land would not be able to supply enough food to nourish all the people and that nothing, save epidemics of disease, famines, or wars, could cut down the growing numbers.

But such melancholy doctrines held little interest for ambitious and enterprising workmen. They would not wait to be cut down by hunger, disease, or enemy bullets. They would leave the country that could not offer them support. They would go to America.

The idea was a brave one, but how were they to get there? The passage was expensive. Most of them had no money.

It was not long before many of them found a way. They found out that American shipmasters, who did a good trade carrying timber, furs, and other raw materials to Europe, needed cargoes for the return voyage. Workingmen bound for America would be the needed ballast. They did not even have to pay their passage: the shipmasters would accept written contracts which provided that the laborers would work for a certain term of years and sign over their wages to pay for their fare across the ocean. The contract was generally written on transparent sheepskin, called vellum, and was torn down the middle. This was called an indenture. The shipmaster kept one half of the indenture and the workingman the other.

It soon appeared that the business of carrying workingmen to America was a very thriving one. Representatives of the shipmasters, called "crimps," combed the English towns to find passengers and traveled through the countryside describing the wonders of America to the credulous, while others, whom people called "newlanders," traveled over to the continent and began talking of America—the land where food was plentiful and a man might own a farm of his own. Women as well as men were invited to sign the contracts, and a great many children were also hauled into the net. Sometimes when a ship's agent could not persuade people to sign up fast enough, they were taken forcibly, carried on board, and kept bound until the vessel was under way. In some of the English cities children were sent from the orphanages to be bound out as servants in the New World. And in others the Privy Council tried sending the inmates of jails—"rogues, vagabonds, and sturdy beggars." But the colonists objected to this—"Abundance of them do great mischief," they said.

The passengers on the little sailing ships were ill

prepared for the miseries of the voyage. They were crowded into dark, ill-ventilated holds, two hundred passengers sometimes being jammed into a space where there was not room for half that number. The food was scarce, the water stagnant. Those who had been "deceived and enticed away" were described as "Crynge and Mourning for Redemption from their Slavery."

Yet on those vessels with all their discomforts and miseries there were vigorous men and women who knew what they were doing. They were ready to start life over again in the New World, and to give their strength and their intelligence to the founding of America.

A crowd of men at the pier greeted the vessels when they landed, and were ready to buy the contracts and to take the newcomers to work for them as servants. The shipping companies, in order that all their cargo might be disposed of, generally advertised in the local newspapers. One such advertisement read:

Just arrived at Leedstown, the Ship *Justitia*, with about one Hundred Healthy Servants.

Men, Women and Boys, among which are Tradespeople —viz. Blacksmiths, Shoemakers, Tailors, House Carpenters, Joiners, a Cooper, several Silversmiths, Weavers, A Jeweler, and many others. The Sale will commence on Tuesday, the 2nd of April at Leeds Town on Rappahannock River. A reasonable credit will be allowed, giving Bond with Approved Security to

Thomas Hodge.

Sometimes, in spite of advertising, the new arrivals were not all placed. Then they were taken to the back country in herds, "like cattle to the Smithfield Market," to be sold at auction.

One historian estimates that about half of all the working people in the colonies came thus as indentured servants and worked a term of years for their freedom.

II

Enter the Merchant Capitalist

Gradually the indentured servants worked out their terms. After they had paid for their passage some of them were given money with which they might buy a piece of land or some tools. Others were paid in pigs or sheep or cattle. Most of them worked from three to five years and then they were free to set up businesses of their own or to work for wages.

People of today might think the life of these working-men crude and hard. John Bach McMaster, the historian, describes the workman's life thus:

Sand sprinkled on the floor did duty as carpet. There was no glass on his table, there was no china in his cupboard, there were no prints on his wall. What a stove was he did not know, coal he had never seen, matches he had never heard of. He rarely tasted fresh meat as often as once in a week, and paid for it a much higher price than did his posterity. . . .

7

If the food of an artisan would now be thought coarse, his clothes would be thought abominable. A pair of yellow buckskin or leathern breeches, a checked shirt, a red flannel jacket, a rusty felt hat cocked up at the corners, shoes of neat's-skin set off with huge buckles of brass, and a leathern apron, comprised his scanty wardrobe. The leather he smeared with grease to keep it soft and flexible.

Such a life seems rough and uncomfortable to us now, but then the rich people of that day did not have many comforts either. And the common laborer, shoemaker, carpenter, printer, or wigmaker had little time for self-pity. For these men were part of a new country—a country free from the burdens and restrictions they had known in Europe. And they were proud of their work and of the delicate skills they had taken years to learn. "An American doubts of nothing," wrote Francis Lieber, a German traveler in this country.

While the rich colonists affected to import their fine suits of clothes and their luxurious furniture from England or France, most of the articles the common people used were made by local craftsmen. These crafts-men worked in their own homes, and generally there was a little farming land around the house where the crafts-man worked in his spare time so that he was not alto-gether dependent on the things he made for his living. However, these articles were in very great demand.

The fast-growing population needed a great many things.

At the door of the craftsman's house a swinging sign bore his name and also a picture of the article he made. The customer walking through the door beneath the sign entered directly into the shop where the craftsman worked. There he found the carpenter with his lathe, or the potter with his wheel, or the shoemaker with his last. Each craftsman owned the tools of his profession and set his own price on the articles he made. He made wigs, shoes, hinges, carriages, or whatever it was, to order. He said they were "bespoken," and he generally had more work than he could do by himself. So sometimes he hired others to help him, and generally he had apprentices in his shop.

These apprentices were boys who were legally bound to him for a certain term. Sometimes the term might be as much as five or six years. The master provided the apprentices with food and shelter and undertook to teach them his craft. They, in return, ran his errands, ground his paints, kept the fire going in his forge, or did whatever tasks he thought he could entrust to them.

When the term of apprenticeship was over, the boys were said to have become journeymen. They could hire themselves out for wages until such time as they could start shops of their own.

In the beginning the work in the craftsmen's shops

was democratic: masters, apprentices, and journeymen felt themselves equal except that some had greater skill than others. They ate their meals together, worked together, and, sometimes, when the work was quiet and monotonous, joined to hire a boy to read to them. Sometimes all the members of a certain craft joined together to form a society which guaranteed certain standards of work or provided benefits for members who were sick, or for funerals. Masters, apprentices, and journeymen all belonged to such societies together.

As the population grew larger and new towns appeared on the American frontiers, it was not always convenient for customers to go to the craftsmen's shops. And so many things were needed now that the leisurely old craftsmen could hardly keep up with the demand. Gradually, then, a new way of working developed.

Now a man appeared who did not make any articles himself; he merely bought and sold them. A merchant capitalist, the historians call him, using a dull term to describe a full-blooded, shrewd man in a beaver hat and ruffled beard.

The merchant capitalist was in fact a trader, a kind of middleman. He did not own any workshop or any tools, nor did he employ any workers. He went about the country buying up articles of every kind—chairs and clocks and spinning wheels, harness and plows and yards of cloth. These he stored in a huge warehouse and later sold to storekeepers at prices higher than he had paid for them. Buy at the cheapest possible rate, he said, sell at the dearest.

The craftsmen, who had been accustomed to set their own prices for the articles they made, now felt the cut of competition. They hired more journeymen and tried to turn out their articles faster. Their shops became, in fact, small factories. And the old spirit of comradeship began to disappear. The master who had to make his products as cheaply as possible tried to cut down on his expenses by paying the journeymen lower wages and making them work faster for longer hours.

This was where the trouble began.

III

A Procession, and a Bright New Day

Pushed on by the demands of the merchant capitalists, American industry began to hum. Toward the middle of the eighteenth century there were little manufacturing plants running in both New England and the Middle Colonies. Some of these were not small but fairly big. Peter Hasenclever, the ironmaster, had a foundry in Pennsylvania to which he brought five hundred workmen from Germany. And Baron Stiegel's glassworks at Mannheim, Pennsylvania, had a plant so large "that a coach and four could turn around within the brick dome of its melting house." One manufacturing house in Boston had hundreds of spinning wheels, and there was a cotton mill in Philadelphia that employed four hundred women to spin cotton thread.

Added to these there were shipyards and ropewalks —those long covered walks where ropes were manufactured—and there were breweries, paper and gunpowder factories. Work needed to be done everywhere. The colonies were like a great anthill with people coming and going, each intent on his own business. There were not enough people to do all the work.

Wages went up—as they do when labor is scarce. The colonial legislatures tried to prevent their rise and to regulate the hours that men should work. The working day should be "10 houres in the daye besides repast," one of them regulated. Another declared it illegal to supplement wages with allowances for liquor, "without which it is found, by too sad experience, many refuse to work." One colonial legislature tried, moreover, to control the way the workingmen dressed. "We declare our utter detestation and dislike," they said, "that men and women of mean condition should take upon themselves the garb of gentlemen."

Despite this snobbery, there was actually more feeling of equality between master and workman in America than there was anywhere in the Old World. Here, it is true, a man could not vote if he did not own property. But in Europe that limitation was taken for granted, whereas in America property qualifications were often questioned.

Many things were being questioned in America now. The control of the colonies by a Parliament that met many miles away across the ocean, the regulations that required the colonies to manufacture certain things and not to manufacture others, the taxes in whose collection and spending the people had no voice. Perhaps what citizens objected to most was the superior attitude of the officials who were placed over them. America, after all, was a good many miles from England. The men who had come here to live were headstrong and independent. They wanted to do things in their own way. It was not hard for them to believe that all men were "created equal," and they were very sure, indeed, that they had a "right to life, liberty, and the pursuit of happiness." When the Declaration of Independence was read out by the officers of the militia in the cities and little towns, they shouted their approval.

It is not easy to go to war, but they did it. They were driven into it by what they regarded as the stupid and intolerable acts of George III's government, by the fiery phrases of Tom Paine's pamphlet, "Common Sense," by their own urge to be independent and free. Master craftsmen, journeymen, apprentices—they all joined with farmers, peddlers, and shopkeepers to make an army. They followed Washington into bloody battles, they trudged along muddy roads, through swamps, across rivers. They were hungry and cold and homesick.

But they knew how to make good guns, and they knew how to shoot them.

When the war at last was over, and the British had sailed away, the farmers went back to their neglected fields and the artisans to the work they had put down. Now the shoemaker could sit down before his last again, the blacksmith could take up the hammer at the forge which had been cold so long, the potter could turn his wheel again. Now nothing could interfere with what they did. Now they were part of a new country, a country that was different from any other in the world. This was to be a country where the people themselves were the masters. Such a government as this had not existed since the days of ancient Greece—that was a good many years ago, the scholars told them.

Through the hot summer of 1788 the leaders of these people sat down to write the Constitution by which this country should be governed. When at last it was finished and nine of the new states adopted it, it became the law of the land. The other four states quickly followed.

There was great rejoicing in America when the Constitution was finally adopted. Everywhere, up and down the eastern seaboard, in cities and towns, in villages and at country crossroads, everywhere that

15

people met, they discussed the new government and the prosperity it would bring. They had been told that the United States was to be a "federal union," that is, that the thirteen states had surrendered their sovereignty and agreed to consolidate themselves into a single new state. The word "federal," therefore, now seemed to be the most popular word in the language. Travelers at country inns now were served mugs of "federal punch," and they smiled with satisfaction as they observed how many men wore "federal" tricorn hats, and smoked "federal" tobacco in "federal" pipes.

Of all the different groups that rejoiced when the new Constitution was adopted none was so jubilant as the craftsmen and artisans. Surely with their skill and their strength and industry they could accomplish extraordinary things, they told each other. They were citizens of a new, free country now.

In Boston, New York, and Philadelphia there were grand processions to celebrate the beginning of the new government. The procession in Philadelphia was the biggest one. There, July 4, 1788, was the day set for the procession in which Philadelphia would celebrate independence and the ratification of the Constitution both at once.

The bells of old Christ Church in Philadelphia began

to ring at dawn that morning, and not long afterward a brisk volley of cannon fire roused up the people.

By eight o'clock a thousand citizens had assembled for the procession; by nine the number had swelled to five thousand. The designated point of assembly was South and Third Streets, but the great crowd spread into all the adjoining streets. Nine marshals on horseback with white plumes on their hats and speaking trumpets in their hands were there to direct them.

By half-past nine they were ready to get under way, and the line of marchers was a mile and a half long. Cheering people crowded the streets as the procession passed, hung from the windows to see it, and leaned precariously from the rooftops. They marched three miles to Union Green, where some fifteen thousand people awaited them and there were speeches and a "collation."

That was a great procession with bands playing and the sun shining and the electricity of hope and excitement firing the marching feet.

The First City Troop, Philadelphia's pride, marched first, and after them other companies of the military, interspersed with bands. Then came the allegorical figure of "Independence," a beautiful young woman drawn along on a cart, another called the "French Alliance," and a figure on horseback representing "George Washington—The Friend of His Country." Then there were more bands and infantry, and then a long, creaking cart in the form of a huge eagle. This cart was drawn by six horses and bore a framed copy of the Constitution fixed on a staff and crowned with a Liberty cap.

Behind the military, behind the bands and the allegory, behind the handsome copy of the Constitution, came the real life of the procession, and the cries of the spectators mounted to a roar as they saw workers and journeymen of every trade, craft, and profession go swinging by. Here walked the architects and house carpenters (four hundred and fifty of them). Then came the Manufacturing Society. They had a carriage thirty feet long on which were a carding machine worked by two persons; a spinning machine of eighty spindles worked by a woman; a lace loom on which a man was weaving a kind of cotton cloth with a fly shuttle. On the cart behind these the people could see an apparatus for printing muslins of an elegant chintz pattern, and a man designing and cutting prints for shawls. These were the latest new devices in the textile industry. The spectators, always eager for new things, watched them pass with noisy admiration.

Behind the textile exhibit marched the shipmasters.

They carried quadrants, trumpets, spyglasses, charts—all the tools of their trade. And they pulled along a model of the ship *Constitution*, decorated lavishly with emblems and beautifully painted.

Now came a great variety of different kinds of workers. The program printed for the occasion gives this list:

Cordwainers (6 men actually making shoes, 300 marching); Coach Painters (10 with palettes and pencils in their hands); Cabinet and Chair makers (a moving workshop with a master, journeyman and apprentices at work); Brick Makers (over a hundred, with a motto: "It was found hard in Egypt, but this prospect"—the new government—"makes it easy."); House, ship and sign makers (68, with equipment for grinding paint); Porters (that is draymen, with five barrels of "Federal flour" which was afterwards delivered to the overseers for the use of the poor); Clock and Watchmakers (24); Fringe and Ribbon Weavers; Bricklayers (masters and workmen with aprons and trowels); Tailors; Instrument Makers; Turners; Windsor Chair and Spinning Wheel Makers (60 in green aprons); Coopers (150 in white leather aprons); Plane Makers; Whip and Cane Manufacturers; Blacksmiths, Whitesmiths and Nailers (over 200, several of them at work on a moving forge).

Coach Makers (150); Potters (a potter's wheel and men at work turning out cups, mugs and bowls); Hatters (125); Wheelwrights (22); Tin Plate Workers; Skinners; Breeches

Makers and Glovers (58 in buckskin breeches and gloves);
Tallow Chandlers carrying a flag with a picture of a chandelier with 13 branches; Victuallers (86 masters, a band of
music and two oxen weighing 3,000 lbs.).

Then:

Fifty Printers, Booksellers and Stationers . . . Saddlers,
Stone Cutters, Bread and Biscuit Makers (130); Gunsmiths,
Coppersmiths, Goldsmiths, Silversmiths, Jewellers, Tobacconists (70); . . . Tanners and Curriers (25 tanners, 35
curriers); Upholsterers; Sugar Refiners in white aprons;
Peruke Makers and Barber Surgeons (72 of them with the
arms of their profession); Plaisterers; Brush Makers.

At the end of the long procession, and enthusiastically
greeted, came the stay makers. They were represented
by Mr. Francis Serre with his first journeyman carrying an elegant pair of ladies' stays.

That was the procession that marched proudly along
the Philadelphia streets, enjoying the cheers of the
onlookers, with the knowledge that a new day had come
to America, that the fighting was over, that the country
was free. They were confident, as one of the patriots
said, that they had a new roof to shelter them—the
sturdy, well-built roof of the Constitution. Beneath that
roof craftsman, journeyman, apprentice, and laborer had
but to carry on the work they knew so well how to do.

A Procession, and a Bright New Day

So in the young republic there were feasting and dancing and high hopes everywhere, because the Constitution had been made and had finally been adopted. At Philadelphia people, going home at last on the night of the great procession, looked up and saw a brilliant aurora borealis lighting the sky. They thought it was a good omen.

IV

Turnouts and Trade Societies

The bright new day the marchers had expected did not come so fast as they had hoped. It was to take long years of patient determination and of struggle to bring the good wages, fair working conditions, and respect which are accepted as the right of American workingmen today.

At the start of the nineteenth century, when the United States was just beginning, the old plan of master craftsmen, apprentices, and journeymen was being gradually replaced by a new one—the merchant capitalist. With his ambitious schemes, his buying and selling, his insistence on the manufacture of large quantities of every article and his lack of interest in their quality, it was the merchant capitalist who seemed responsible for changing the old ways, though there were some who claimed that it was a natural evolution—that the methods of industry were changing only because the country was growing so fast.

The cost of living in the United States was rising very fast in the early 1800's. Journeymen in every trade felt the pinch, for their wages were being cut to meet the demand for cheap manufactured articles, yet food and rent were higher than ever. In the newspapers of the time you will find advertisements explaining their predicament. Here is one published by the journeymen printers in the *Royal Gazette:*

As the necessaries of life are raised to such an enormous price, it cannot be expected that we should continue to work at the wages now given; and therefore request an addition of Three Dollars per week to our small pittance; it may be objected that this requisition is founded upon the result of a combination to distress the Master Printers at this time, on account of the scarcity of hands; but this is far from being the case, it really being the high price of every article of life, added to the approaching dreary season. There is not one among us, we trust, that would take an ungenerous advantage of the times—we only wish barely to exist, which it is impossible to do with our present stipend.

If the master printers read the advertisement in the *Royal Gazette*, they did not pay much attention. Neither did the masters in other trades pay much heed to their men who wished barely to exist—to the cabinet-makers, shoemakers, metalworkers, and others who found it impossible to manage on the wages paid them.

Since the masters would not listen to the pleas of individual workers, or even to small groups of them, the journeymen began looking for some way to make them listen. If they could get all the men in a certain trade to join together in a single group, and if these men refused to work unless adequate wages were paid them, then the masters would have to listen, they believed.

The idea of a strike, or a "turnout" as it was then called, was not a new one. There had been a good many turnouts before the Revolution. The men had stayed home from work until a settlement was reached and then gone back to work. They disapproved of violence, though sometimes it occurred. Once a group of seamen paraded through a Philadelphia street demanding higher wages. They were noisy and rowdy, and the constabulary had to break up the procession. Everyone thought this a disgrace.

There was some disorder too when the journeyman cordwainers, or shoemakers, turned out in an effort to get more pay. Six of these men had continued to work for the old wages, and the master of the shop hid them in his house. But on a Sunday night, when these six slipped out to go to a nearby tavern, the journeymen who had turned out set on the six. There was a bloody fight and all decent and law-abiding citizens were horrified.

These incidents were the exception rather than the rule, for almost all turnouts were conducted in an orderly fashion. Nevertheless, public opinion was strongly against "trade societies," as unions of workmen were then called. Because of this the more timid refused to join them—the bolder often joined them anyway but kept the fact secret.

Soon trade societies were growing up in almost every kind of work. These societies held regular meetings but the members swore to keep their proceedings secret. They swore also that they would not reveal who the members were. Initiation fees in the societies were generally fifty cents, and dues varied from five to eight cents a month. The members swore that they would not work for wages below a certain rate, and that they would turn out when the majority of the members so voted. Any man who refused to join in the turnout was called a "scab," a term of great scorn.

The members of the trade societies tried to help each other to get work. They tried also to make the masters employ only those who belonged to their number— that is, they tried to have what is called today a "closed shop."

The courts of the time reflected the strong public

sentiment against the trade societies. This made it go hard with the workers if any of them were tried, and indeed in nearly every trial involving members of trade societies the judgment was against the workingman. An example of this was the case of *The Commonwealth of Pennsylvania* vs. *the Cordwainers*, which was tried in Philadelphia in March, 1806.

Twelve small businessmen composed the jury that tried the cordwainers. Three of them were innkeepers, and among the others were a merchant, a watchmaker, a tobacconist, a hatter, a tailor, and a bottler.

These men listened gravely to the accusation brought against the accused. According to the court record: first, they had attempted "to increase and augment the prices usually paid them"; second, they had "attempted to prevent other workmen and journeymen in their occupation from working except for certain large sums . . ."; and third, they had "deceitfully formed themselves into a club to attain their ends. . . ."

Now according to the charge which the judge made to the jury there was nothing illegal about a man asking for more money or even in his trying to influence the amount paid to others. But for men to join themselves together to try to attain these ends was a "conspiracy" and therefore illegal.

It was on these grounds that the eight shoemakers, tried before the bar that day, were found guilty and fined. This case set a precedent on which other cases were decided.

Not until 1842 did trade societies become legal. Then Chief Justice Lemuel Shaw of Massachusetts held that unions were legal as long as they sought to achieve lawful ends. Though this was an important decision, the public still held the unions in high disapproval.

Though the attitude of the general public and of the courts was discouraging it did not prevent new trade societies from forming. There were turnouts of tailors in Buffalo, of ship carpenters in Philadelphia, and cabinetmakers in Baltimore; and also of journeyman painters, tailors, stonecutters, and even common laborers in New York. Up in Pawtucket, Rhode Island, where water-driven textile mills were beginning to operate, the woman weavers decided on a turnout. [The turnout] "was conducted, strange as it may appear, without noise, and with scarcely a single speech."

By about 1820 local societies seemed to be springing up everywhere. The next step was the joining together of a number of these societies. And so in Philadelphia in 1827, the Mechanics Union of Trade Associations was formed. It was the first labor organization which brought workers of several crafts together in one association.

The carpenters of Philadelphia had struck that year for a ten-hour day. They said, "All men have a just right derived from their Creator to have sufficient time in each day for the cultivation of their minds and for self-improvement." Other members of the building trades—the bricklayers, painters, and glaziers—also wanted time for the "cultivation of their minds," and supported the carpenters. The strike did not succeed, but the idea persisted that if a large enough number of unions banded together they might succeed. And those craftsmen who had no societies were urged to organize. The members of the Mechanics Union dreamed that they might accomplish far more than simply a ten-hour day. They drew up a constitution for their society and in it they wrote:

If the mass of people were enabled by their labor to procure for themselves and families a full and abundant supply of the comforts and conveniences of life, the consumption of articles, particularly of dwellings, furniture, and clothing, would amount to at least twice the quantity it does at present, and of course the demand, by which the employers are enabled to subsist or accumulate, would likewise be increased in an equal proportion. . . .

Many years later Henry Ford, turning out automobiles by mass-production methods, discovered this same idea. He believed that if the workingman was paid enough to buy the goods he made in large quantity, the country as a whole would prosper. But it was to be many years before this truth was understood.

Meantime, the Mechanics Union looked about for ways of using its new-found strength. It believed that it might exert its greatest influence by way of politics.

V

The Workingmen's Parties Have Ideas

Since colonial times American workingmen had wanted to vote. Only a man who owned land, or who possessed a certain amount of money, was admitted to the polls. New Jersey was the first state to alter this. She gave the vote to all white males in 1807. Maryland followed in 1810, and after that the other states. The conservatives worried when this happened. What was to become of the United States now? they asked.

Labor leaders were quick to grasp the new power that had been put into their hands. If every man could vote, why should workingmen not run for office, and why should they not be elected? Great things might be accomplished with their representatives in office. The Mechanics Union lost no time in communicating with its members in every state. Form workingmen's parties, it urged. Elect labor candidates.

So the workingmen's parties were organized and

labor candidates named, and sixty-eight labor newspapers explaining the new party policies came rolling off the presses. George Henry Evans, a printer by trade, published one of the best of these newspapers in New York. It was called *The Working Man's Advocate.* The labor press pointed out that with the vote candidates who favored labor's cause could be elected. Labor might even put up candidates of its own.

There were many things in the United States that they wanted to change: they hardly knew where to begin. But they agreed that lack of education was what hindered them most. Their children were "being brought up as ignorant as the Arabs of the desert," they said.

How could a man be a good citizen unless he could at least read and write? They did not want to go to charity schools and they could not afford the expensive private schools the rich attended. They wanted free schools for everybody and they wanted them supported by taxes.

It was true, as the labor press pointed out, that a large percentage of the people in the United States had had no education at all. In Pennsylvania 250,000 children out of 400,000 had never been to school. In the country as a whole more than a million people were totally illiterate. How can you have a true democracy where the people cannot read and write? It was not strange that workingmen spoke of education almost reverently: they called it "the greatest blessing bestowed on mankind."

"There can be no liberty without a wide diffusion of knowledge," the editor of a labor paper wrote. "The members of a republic should all be alike instructed in the nature and character of their equal rights and duties as human beings and as citizens."

The labor press pointed out, too, that attendance at school would make the future citizens law-abiding and cut down the amount of delinquency; that it would make them responsible citizens.

The rich and conservative objected to the idea of "Universal, Equal Education." Why should we be taxed to support the schools where mechanics and laborers go? they asked.

But the workers succeeded. Their success was one of the great achievements in American history. Pennsylvania was the first state to adopt a program of tax-supported schools and other states soon followed her example.

Education was not the only thing the workers wanted. They wanted to abolish debtors' prisons. At that time hundreds of poor men were thrown into prison for debt. Once there, they had no way of earning money to get out again. According to one report 750,000 people were imprisoned for debt every year. Half of these people owed less than $25 and many of them as little as $1.00. The prisons were crowded, dirty, and unsanitary, and no food was provided for the inmates. Those imprisoned for debt had to depend on family and friends for food, though those who had committed criminal offenses were provided for by the state.

"A law which makes poverty a crime and a poor man a felon . . . is not only cruel and oppressive, but absurd and revolting," one man wrote.

But here again the workingmen succeeded. First they managed to have prisoners for debt released if they took an oath of bankruptcy; then they got a limit set to the amount of debt for which a man might be imprisoned. And, finally, the debtors' jails were done away with altogether.

The militia system was another matter in which labor took a great interest, for every man was required then to attend frequent drills and parades, which generally lasted off and on for three days. And every man was required to pay for his own uniform and equipment. He lost his wages on the days he served, so the burden appeared very heavy. Added to this, failure to comply with the requirements of the militia meant a fine or imprisonment—a fine which it was not hard for the rich man to pay but which bore heavily on the poor man.

Because the militia service was so hard on workingmen they fought against it through their press and through their political parties. And here, too, they were successful. After 1830 militia laws were altered or abolished in almost every state.

The workingmen's parties were burning with enthusiasm for what they had accomplished, and now they pressed on to right what they considered another wrong. Now they gathered their forces to pass Mechanics Lien Laws. They had discovered that when an employer went into bankruptcy he did not pay back wages. This sometimes meant that the worker lost from one to six months' pay. A man whose wages make it necessary for him to live close to the edge of hunger cannot afford to lose even a single day's pay. The workingmen's parties set to work to have laws passed by which the employer was required to pay the wages he owed before he paid his other debts. Here, too, they succeeded. The Mechanics Lien Laws have been in existence ever since.

The business interests of the country were alarmed by the power of the workingmen's parties, with all their ideas and all their successes. The *Journal of Commerce* wrote indignantly: "By throwing open the polls to every man that walks power was placed in the hands of those who had neither property, talents nor influence in other circumstances."

The storm against the workingmen's parties grew more and more turbulent. Businessmen, newspapers, and the members of the major political parties joined together and organized a great campaign to crush them. Employers threatened to discharge any man who was a member of a workers' party, and they carried out their threats. Newspapers printed articles attacking them as "radical" and spoke of their members as the "mob," the "rag, tag, and bobtail."

Inside the parties themselves the leadership was inexperienced and uncertain. The members of the workingmen's parties were for the most part skilled craftsmen, but there were hundreds of others—common laborers, workers in the new factories, women and children—who were not represented in the workingmen's parties at all.

Perhaps what finally put an end to the movement was Andrew Jackson. "Andy" was the friend of the workingman—his re-election in 1832 was proof of their trust in him. They united solidly behind him and forgot the workingmen's parties.

Though the workingmen's parties no longer existed,

the work that they had done remained. The American public schools, the abolition of debtors' prisons, the modification of the militia laws, the Mechanics Lien Laws—the benefits of every reform the workers fought for in the 1820's are in existence today.

VI

What Building the Railroads Meant

The building of the railroads changed America from an agricultural country to a great industrial one. Before their coming America had been a land of farms and small seaboard cities, a land where water-driven and later steam-powered machinery was beginning to replace the old hand-powered machines, where merchant capitalists were trying to find wider markets for manufactured goods.

There were no really big cities in America before the railroads were built, no great industries, no slums, no mass unemployment. Then the railroads were built, and all these things came with them.

John Stevens of Hoboken, New Jersey, experimented with a railroad first in 1820. He built a circular wooden track in the grounds of Castle Point, his place in Hoboken. Then he built a kind of locomotive and attached a carriage to it. Sitting in this carriage, he drove around and around the track with great satisfaction. It appeared to him that travel by railroad would be much more satisfactory than going along the old turnpikes in wagons or coaches, much quicker than going by waterway up and down rivers and through canals. John Stevens had been in close touch with England and he knew that railroads had been in use there for a good many years. He thought it would not be necessary for the government to subsidize the building of the new railroads as they had the turnpikes and the canals. Railroads could be built by the initiative of private businessmen. He believed that they could soon be made to pay for themselves.

The Baltimore and Ohio was the first American railroad. On July 4, 1828, Charles Carroll of Carrollton, the last living signer of the Declaration of Independence, officiated at the laying of the first B. and O. track. A whole network of other railroad tracks was soon to follow. People were moving across the Appalachians then, opening up new lands in Ohio, Indiana, and Illinois. The railroads were a direct though not very comfortable way to get there.

Those early railroads used wood to fire their boilers. Each locomotive had a little platform on which the logs were piled and a man rode along to heave the wood into the furnace under the boiler. A big plume of black smoke rolled back behind the train as it rattled along, and the sparks went shooting up, setting fire to the roofs of buildings along the way and burning holes in the clothes of the passengers. The cars in which those passengers bumped along were like a string of little carriages hitched together. They were gaily painted in bright colors, as was the locomotive itself.

The progress of the trains was uncertain. At first they ran on wooden tracks, but these were not generally strong enough to bear the weight of the moving cars, and when they were crushed it was necessary to stop and put down another track. So it was not long before the railroad managers began to use iron rails. These buckled and broke sometimes, and pieces of them stuck through the floor of the cars. Thanks to Andrew Carnegie, steel rails were used at last. Wooden bridges, too, were replaced with iron ones, and then with bridges of steel.

As the years passed, more and more railroad trains went shrieking over the hills and through the valleys, across rivers and through mountain passes. Gangs of Irishmen, who had come to America to escape the potato famines, worked at laying the tracks.

The building of the railroads did much more than carry settlers to lands across the Appalachians, though this in fact they did. When tracks were made of iron and then of steel, large quantities of those metals were needed. The iron foundries which had served since colonial days were no longer adequate to make the tracks and bridges that were needed. Soon blast furnaces were roaring, and Bessemer converters were pouring the molten metal into molds. Great numbers of unskilled workers were needed in the steel plants now, and steel manufacturers, since they could not find enough unskilled laborers in America, were sending to Europe to entice workers to this country. Industry on a vast scale was booming in the steel mills.

But that was not all. Iron in the old days had been made by burning out the impurities in iron ore with charcoal. Now coal was used. New fields of bituminous coal were uncovered in Pennsylvania and West Virginia, and more men were brought from overseas to dig the coal from underground. Coal mining was a dirty, difficult job, and a dangerous one, with frequent cave-ins, explosions, and poisonous gases. The American workmen did not like to work in the steel mills, but they liked even less to work in the mines. The mine operators brought labor from abroad. The immigrant workmen wanted less pay, anyway.

Just as the building of the railroads had brought about the creation of the steel mills and the digging of the coal mines, they were responsible for the fast growth of the American cities. They could carry goods wherever they were needed: they could carry raw materials to the factories, and manufactured articles to populations that lived far away. They could bring the farmers' produce to the city dwellers who hardly knew a rake from a hoe or a plow from a tractor. Grain, loads of pigs, sheep, and cattle, all came pouring into the city markets to be bought by the city workers with the wages they had earned.

The American workingmen hated the changes that had come to America. They hated the steel mills that roared all night and all day. They hated the dirty coal mines. They saw slums growing up in their cities where crowds of the foreign-born lived in dilapidated and unsanitary surroundings. They thought the immigrants would lower the whole standard of American life. They hated the changes the railroads had brought to America —but what could they do?

There were a good many intelligent and visionary men and women in America in the middle of the nineteenth century who were interested in workingmen's problems and eager to help them. Arthur Brisbane, editor of the *New York Tribune*, urged the building of "phalanxes," or communities where rich and poor, scholars, craftsmen, and laborers all lived together, each contributing whatever skill he possessed. The plan had been worked out originally by a Frenchman named Fourier, and Arthur Brisbane and his friends succeeded in establishing forty-three such communities in America. But they did not last.

There were some who tried to form cooperative societies, selling the things they produced themselves. "The directions and profits of industry must be kept in the hands of the producers," they said.

The Working Man's Advocate wanted to persuade Congress to give land away free to anyone who applied for it. Its editor thought that this would relieve the pressure of excess population in the cities and make it possible for those who were discontented with things as they were to start a new life. This idea was actually put into practice when the Homestead Act of 1862 was passed. Some thought that matters were improved by it, but others pointed to the fact that many workingmen did not want to go West, had not capital to invest in fences and farm implements and buildings, and did not know how to farm anyway.

Whatever the solution, the railroads were bringing America great changes and great problems—problems and changes that were talked of everywhere in the United States. Those who were most thoughtful believed the problems could not be solved by utopian schemes. Somehow, within the vast framework of the new industry, a way must be found for employer and employee to work together for their common good. It was to take years for this way to be found. There was to be bitterness and violence before capital and labor learned to work together. They have not learned that way completely yet.

VII

William Sylvis of the Iron Molders Union

━━━━━━━━━━━━━━━━━━━━━━━

Utopias and visionary plans, cooperatives, phalanxes, free land, and political parties—none of them
accomplished much for working people, though everywhere in the districts where the workingmen lived they
talked about these things. Men saw that prices were
steadily going up but wages did not rise in proportion.
They saw the problems that they faced frequently discussed in the newspapers. The *New York Times* said:
"Each spring witnesses a new struggle for enhanced
wages in some if not most of the trades of this and other
cities." And the Trenton *Daily State Gazette* said:
"Men should always have a fair compensation for their
labor."

Men should indeed have a fair compensation for their
labor, but how were they to get it? The thoughtful

among them believed there was no way save by forming themselves into unions. The voice of an individual man could hardly be heard in a great industry. Generally he did not even see the men who were responsible for paying his wages. Joined with his fellows in a union, though, with the power to strike if that became necessary, he had a chance to be heard.

In the districts where the workingmen lived, they talked about these facts after their work was done, puffing the smoke up slowly from their pipes. In more and more places they organized unions.

Membership in the unions at that time was confined to skilled craftsmen. Unskilled immigrant labor was not admitted; neither were women allowed to join.

Before very long local unions of painters, plumbers, carpenters, iron molders, shipwrights, longshoremen, and locomotive engineers were formed. Many of these unions decided to go on strike, and some of these strikes were successful, though many of them were not. The local unions did not generally have enough money to keep a strike going long. If only the unions could be organized with a national union treasury, the men would stand a much better chance.

William H. Sylvis of the Iron Molders Union was one of the first to realize the importance of having national unions. The son of a wagonmaker in Annoph, Pennsylvania, he had been apprenticed in an iron foundry. He finished his apprenticeship and became a journeyman molder some time before 1850. The terms of his agreement provided that on becoming a journeyman he was to be given a fine broadcloth suit, white shirt, woolen hose, calfskin boots, and a high silk hat. So equipped, he was ready to start his career.

But William Sylvis's fine clothes apparently did not make much impression on him. It is doubtful whether he wore them long, for he had other things on his mind.

He wanted to strengthen the Iron Molders Union—to increase its membership. And then, as he thought more about it, he wanted to make it a national organization of many unions.

Sylvis was in earnest in his belief that unions should be organized on a national scale. As soon as he could he left the foundry where he had worked and began to travel from one city to another. Everywhere he stopped he met groups of molders, discussed how they could best organize, and encouraged them to join the national union.

"Those were the happiest years of my life," he said afterward. He traveled through New England and the seaboard states, and then went on into the Midwest and

Canada. It was wonderful to him to see the unions grow. "The National Iron Molders Union has grown from a pygmy to a giant," he wrote later. After a time he persuaded the iron molders to form locals in Canada. After the Canadian workers joined, it was called the International Molders Union.

He had very little money for his traveling. Sometimes he persuaded the engineer of a train to let him ride free in the locomotive's cab. His clothes grew more and more shabby as he went, but he hardly noticed that. His brother wrote later:

"He wore clothes until they were quite threadbare and he could wear them no longer. The shawl he wore to the day of his death . . . was filled with little holes burned there by the splashing of molten metal from the ladles of molders in strange cities whom he was beseeching to organize."

"I love this union cause," Sylvis once said. "I hold it more dearly than I do my family or my life. I am willing to devote to it all that I am, or have, or hope for in the world."

He talked in this vein wherever he went, and people everywhere listened. "His name has become a household word," the New York *Sun* reported.

So the Iron Molders Union grew larger and more

powerful, and thousands of names were added to its rolls.

Now the country was torn by the Civil War, and in the North the workingmen put down their tools to join the army. And when the war was over those who came back to work faced the same old problems.

Only the problems now seemed greater. New factories seemed to have sprung up everywhere during the war—factories to make cloth for uniforms, to make shoes and hats and all manner of other things. Immigrant labor was being imported in great quantities. In 1864 a contract labor law had been passed by which companies were allowed to advance passage money to immigrants which they could repay gradually from their wages. Besides the immigrants there were the Negroes. Four million of them, freed from slavery, had come North to look for work. The old skilled craftsmen of former days looked with hostility at both immigrants and Negroes. They were bringing down the standards of all working-men, they said.

But there were more difficulties than simply the competition of immigrants and Negroes. In the years immediately following the Civil War industrial America had come into its own. The railroad tracks had been laid all the way to the Pacific coast, and subsidiary lines ran back and forth and up and down. New towns had been built along the railroad, and telegraph wires kept one distant place in touch with another. Oil had been discovered in Titusville, Pennsylvania, and the big blast furnaces were lighting up the skies over Pittsburgh, while the stockyards at Chicago were booming. E. H. Harriman, Jay Gould, Andrew Carnegie, and John D. Rockefeller were laying the foundations of vast fortunes.

The ruthless industrialists of that time thought of labor as a commodity to be bought and sold. What chance would labor have with industry organized on a vast scale unless labor was organized on a vast scale, too? William Sylvis was one of the first to believe that American labor should form itself into one great body if it was to protect what he believed to be its rights and privileges.

Under the inspiration of William Sylvis, therefore, seventy-seven delegates from various unions met in Baltimore in 1866 to form the National Labor Union. A big banner hung in the convention hall bearing the words "Welcome to the Sons of Toil from North, East, South and West." It was the first labor meeting on a national scale in American history.

William Sylvis was absent from the first meetings of the National Labor Union, but when he finally appeared the delegates applauded as he stepped to the center of the flag-draped platform and told them of the plans and ambitions he had built up through the years. He wore his customary shabby clothes and the worn cape that was peppered with holes.

Sylvis spoke of organizing a Department of Labor in the federal government, of trying to restrict immigration, and of abolishing convict labor. He spoke of trying to have grants of free land in the West limited to those who would actually settle there. And then he spoke of the eight-hour day.

"We ought to start to work for the eight-hour day," he said. "But we ought not to try to get it by strikes." For William Sylvis, perhaps because he had had some bitter experiences as the result of a strike of the molders union, disliked strikes. They were too hard on the men and too costly, and they did not succeed in the long run, he believed. Labor ought to get what it wanted by law. Labor ought to use its influence to get the government to pass an eight-hour law.

The place of women in industry was another matter that had cost him much thought. Women ought to be paid the same wages as men for equal work, he maintained. And there was the matter of the Negroes, who were willing to work for much lower wages than did the white man. Sylvis would doubtless have asked them to join the unions, but he knew that racial prejudice against them was too strong. He urged that the Negroes form unions of their own.

The advances that Sylvis urged were slow in coming, and he felt that there must be some more fundamental way of doing away with poverty and bringing men what he considered their due. So he turned back to the idea of cooperatives, which had been tried in the 1840's. Let laboring men own the business in which they worked. By forming cooperatives they could get what they considered their fair share of the profits.

But it takes money to start a cooperative. And where was the bank that would lend money to labor? The currency system of the country ought to be reformed, he said, in answer to that question. More paper money should be printed and distributed so that people could have more of it.

So William Sylvis's ideas changed. From the eight-hour day and equality of women he had gone on to urging the formation of cooperatives and monetary reform.

And the people, listening to this man who was seeking so earnestly to find a way to help workingmen, followed him. They changed the National Labor Union into the National Labor and Reform party, and just as they had failed when they tried to go into politics before, so they failed now. By 1872 the National Labor and Reform party no longer existed.

But though Sylvis's new party had melted like a spring snow under a warm sun, what they had done was not altogether in vain. For a brief time they had held together 600,000 members. In 1868 they succeeded in having a law passed that provided for an eight-hour day for government employees. And the shorter working day was later brought to most other employees.

But the experience of the National Labor and Reform party pointed out that labor could not succeed in American politics—at least not in the nineteenth century.

In 1872 it might have seemed as if the national labor movement was a failure. But it had moved perhaps two feet forward and one foot back.

VIII

The Ugly Face of Violence

Depression swept across the country in the 1870's. Banks closed, and profits fell off in almost every industry, while factories, mines, and mills shut down and four million unemployed men and women tramped the streets looking for work. There had been unemployment in America before, but never anything like this. In city after city men and women were homeless, hungry, and in despair. In New York, Chicago, Boston, Cincinnati, and Omaha great mass meetings of the unemployed were held.

The biggest of those mass meetings was held on January 13, 1874, in New York City. Thousands of men and women crowded into Tompkins Square that day, seeking to demonstrate to the city authorities that they needed relief. They had had permission from the city to hold the meeting, and had in fact been told that the mayor would come to address them. The square was packed with people waiting to hear what he would say.

At the last minute, however, there was a change of plans. The authorities had learned that a man whom they believed to be an anarchist was to address the meeting. So permission to hold the meeting was canceled, and the police were ordered to clear the square.

Ruthlessly now the mounted police charged the crowd, swinging their clubs, and men, women, and children ran before the advancing horses. Some of the crowd were trampled; some were clubbed, and scores were injured.

The young Samuel Gompers, a cigar maker, watched as the police drove the crowd before them. He dodged into a cellarway for safety.

"I saw how radicalism could hurt labor's cause," he said years afterward. He was to become a great force in the labor movement, but always a conservative one.

As the mass meetings continued in one city after another, people looked at the unemployed more and more fearfully, saying that their discontent was being stirred up by foreign agitators. No one seemed to understand that empty stomachs could be responsible for rioting.

Unemployment in the industrial centers was not the only difficulty that afflicted America in the 1870's. There were struggles between workers and their employers

"Between the Strike and the Family." Before there were national union treasuries, many strikes failed for lack of money. Above, a worker is torn between the pleadings of fellow-workers and his family. *Harper's Weekly*, 1872.

The first major depression swept across the country in the 1870's. Below, homeless men sleep in a New York police station. Winslow Homer drawing from *Harper's Weekly*.

As police arrived to disperse workers listening to radical speeches at Haymarket Square, Chicago, during the eight-hour day movement in 1886, an unknown person threw a bomb and the peaceful gathering turned into a riot. *Harper's Weekly.*

This 1886 cartoon, a play on the name of the second leader of the Knights of Labor, Terence V. Powderly, was captioned, "There is a great deal in his name, and a great responsibility in the way in which he guards it." Thomas Nast in *Harper's Weekly.*

Samuel Gompers headed the American Federation of Labor every year but one from its founding in 1886 until his death in 1924 and thus shaped the policy of American organized labor for nearly forty years. This photograph was taken in 1910. Bettmann Archive.

Pinkerton men, hired to protect strike breakers during the steel strike at Homestead, Pa., in 1892, were captured by the strikers after a gun battle and are here shown on the way to their temporary prison. *Harper's Weekly.*

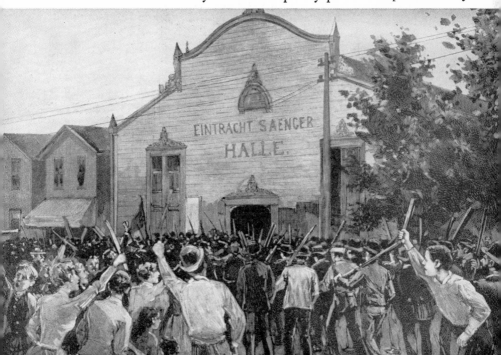

The injunction was used to break the Pullman Strike of 1894 and federal troops were sent to enforce it. The strike had completely tied up the railroads and cut off supplies to city markets. Above, the first meat train leaves the Chicago stockyards under escort of U.S. Cavalry. *Harper's Weekly*.

Eugene Debs, shown below addressing railroad workers in 1912, led the American Railway Union during the Pullman Strike of 1894. He and three other union officials were imprisoned for disobeying an injunction. Brown Brothers.

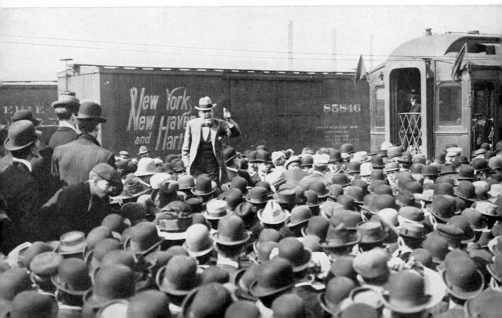

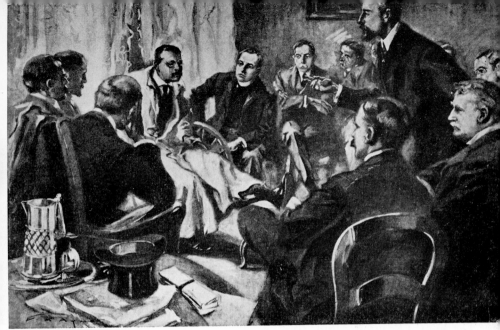

President Theodore Roosevelt (in light coat) called this meeting of mine operators and union representatives during the coal strike of 1902. The operators later agreed to arbitration after pressure by the President. John Mitchell, president of United Mine Workers, is at Roosevelt's left, leaning forward. *Harper's Weekly.*

Industrial Workers of the World organizers spoke on street corners and handed out cards like this one. Note that aims include both "more wages" and "abolition of the wage system." The I.W.W. was founded in 1905 and lost its influence during World War I. Courtesy of the New York Public Library.

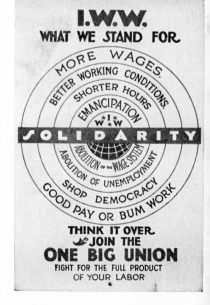

The Works Progress Administration during the depression years of 1935 to 1942 employed some 8,500,000 persons, thus saving their self-respect and providing many useful and lasting public works. Above, WPA workers build a New Jersey home and hospital for afflicted children in 1938. Wide World Photo.

The Fair Labor Standards Act of 1938 put an end to child labor in firms dealing in interstate commerce. Below is a "carrying-in-boy" in a Virginia glass factory in 1911. Lewis W. Hine photo from the Jacob Riis Collection, Museum of the City of New York.

William Green (left), leader of the A.F.L., talks to John L. Lewis, head of the C.I.O., in 1940 in an attempt to bring the two groups together again. Both were sons of Welsh miners and had worked in the mine pits as boys, but their ideas on union organization differed. International News Photo.

Walter Reuther, president of the United Automobile Workers, signs the first guaranteed annual wage agreement in 1955. Beside him at the head of the table is John Bugas, Ford Motor Company vice-president. United Automobile Worker photo.

George Meany, first president of the newly merged A.F.L.-C.I.O., addresses the delegates at the 1955 national convention. By this time labor had grown strong—more than eighteen million Americans carried union cards. *The AFL-CIO News.*

in several industries, and notably in the coal mines and on the railroads.

The strike of 1874-1875 in the coal mines has since been called the "Long Strike." It occurred when the Pennsylvania operators decided to cut the men's wages, thus breaking the union contract. Then all through the Pennsylvania coal regions miners stayed home from work: the pits were quiet. The strike dragged on week after week. But a man can go without his wages only so long. And the union had not enough funds to support the strikers indefinitely. Gradually here and there miners began trickling back into the mines again.

Those who held out were bitter against the returning miners, and tried to prevent them from entering the mine shafts. Then the operators hired armed guards called "coal and iron police" to defend the strikebreakers. This enraged the strikers and soon there was a shooting war.

Now, as if things were not bad enough, another element entered the conflict. Many of the miners were Irish and the rumor got abroad that there were terrorists among them. It was known that there was a secret society in Ireland called the Ancient Order of Hibernians, which had been formed by Irish tenants to terrorize their landlords. One of the leading spirits in the Ancient

Order was a woman named Molly Maguire. So people now spoke of the members of the society as the Molly Maguires.

It was suspected that the Molly Maguires might be threatening the coal operators, their superintendents and foremen, and the men who had gone back to work. A man from the Pinkerton Detective Agency was hired to mingle with the men and collect evidence, and before long twenty-four were accused and convicted of terrorism. Of these twenty-four, ten were hanged and the others sentenced to jail terms.

Intimidated by such harsh measures, the miners' union was broken up, the miners went back to work, and there was order in the mines again. But recent historians, basing their judgment on later careful research, doubt whether the Molly Maguires were really active in the mines at all.

Peace had hardly been restored in the coal mines when trouble broke out on the railroads. For, although the directors had recently voted an 8 per cent dividend for their stockholders, they announced, in 1877, that they were about to cut the wages of the railroad men. That made violent trouble.

The men of the Baltimore and Ohio Railroad reacted first when news of the wage cut came, and they went on strike immediately. The Pennsylvania, New York Central, and Erie railroad men followed suit, and soon the railroad lines of the whole country east of the Mississippi were tied up.

Now at Martinsburg, West Virginia, the strikers of the B. and O. line stopped all the trains and seized railroad property. So the governor of West Virginia sent the militia to protect the railroad property, and the strikers greeted them with stones and brickbats. The militiamen, overpowered, ran to take refuge in the railroad station, and the strikers surrounded the station and set fire to it. When police and firemen came to put out the fire, the strikers tried to prevent them but finally gave in. All night the rioting lasted, and when morning came nine persons were dead and many injured. Three of the injured later died.

Events at Martinsburg were repeated in other places. Strikers seized trains and railroad property in Pittsburgh, but the militia, who were sent to subdue them, refused to shoot at their fellow townsmen.

Then a federal force of 650 soldiers was sent to Pittsburgh, and they opened fire. The crowd of strikers now had swelled to four or five thousand people, for they had been joined by idlers and tramps and others. Infuriated when the troops fired, this crowd tore up the railroad tracks, burned the roundhouse, broke open freight and passenger cars. That night about two thousand cars, a grain elevator, and two roundhouses with one hundred and twenty-five locomotives went up in flames, and the Union Depot was burned down. Looting and rioting were added to the fires as the unruly elements in the city now took advantage of the situation. Some of the citizens tried to help the police restore order, and later the entire state militia was called out.

But it was not until more federal troops had been sent by President Hayes that order was finally restored. Between five and ten million dollars' worth of property had been destroyed, and the number of casualties is not known.

That was the pattern in city after city, until finally the fire of resentment against the railroad operators burned out. The workers knew they could do nothing against the United States Army, and they, too, hated violence. So by the end of July the trains were running again, and the men had gone back to work.

Newspaper headlines throughout America expressed horror at what had been happening. They pointed out that the working people had been thoroughly beaten, that the miners' union had been destroyed, and the railroad strikes crushed. Yet they noted that the employers, too, had seen the ugly face of violence. There would be another way of settling disagreements between employers and employed but no one, at the end of the 1870's, had yet found it. It would be a long time before that way was discovered.

IX

Foreigners?

Those who had seen the great mass meetings of the hungry and desperate unemployed, who had heard sinister stories of the Molly Maguires and seen railroad men tearing up tracks and burning cars, were thoroughly frightened. America must be on the verge of revolution, they thought. They could not believe that Americans would commit such acts of violence. They laid the blame on "foreigners."

It is true that there were some anarchists in the great flood of Europeans who were landing in America. Bitter because of what they had experienced in Europe, they continued to preach revolution in this country. One of the most prominent was a big, black-bearded German named Johann Most. Chicago appeared to be a center for such radicals. There were eight anarchist newspapers there, seven of them in foreign languages. In Chicago, likewise, the anarchists had formed an organization, called the International Working People's Association.

Active as these few anarchists were, however, they had little influence on Americans. For Americans, though they were eager to better their condition in any way they could, to get better pay and to work shorter hours, had not the least idea of upsetting their government. They were proud of America and loyal to it. The foreign agitators did not accomplish much.

Nevertheless, the American public kept blaming the foreign agitators for the labor troubles. How else could they be explained? they asked. Somehow these radicals must be stamped out. Then the country would go back to its peaceful ways again.

This was wrong, of course. The difficulty lay much deeper than they understood. The difficulty was that the great industrialized society had not yet learned how to deal with mass unemployment or adjustments of wages and hours. Americans had not even begun to understand such complicated matters. How much simpler to blame all the trouble on the foreign agitators.

The opportunity for making an example of the foreign agitators soon presented itself. There had been a widespread series of strikes for the eight-hour day on May 1, 1886. At one of these demonstrations, which was called at the McCormick harvester machine plant in Chicago, there was a clash between the strikers and the police. Four men were killed.

The radicals promptly called on the working people of Chicago to hold a meeting the next day in Haymarket Square. About three thousand people answered their call and stood in the square listening to speeches. The mayor of Chicago had gone to the meeting to watch the proceedings, and the police were held in readiness in case there should be violence. But nothing happened. It was a dull meeting.

The speeches were still going on when a cold wind began to blow and rain beat down. The people scattered. "There's no use of staying any longer," the mayor said, and he, too, went home.

There were only a scattering of about five hundred people left in the square when a group of police appeared and began breaking up what remained of the crowd.

Suddenly there was a sharp explosion. Someone had hurled a bomb into the ranks of the police. The police opened fire on the crowd. The people fired back.

Now there was a confusion of pistol shots, and men shouting, and people trying to run away. When the smoke had cleared and the square was quiet again seven policemen were dead and about sixty-seven injured. Four of the workers had been killed and fifty hurt.

And no one knew who had thrown the bomb: no one knows to this day. But the whole country was aroused by what had happened in Haymarket Square. The anarchists must be made an example of. If they were brought to justice, the labor troubles would come to an end.

So the anarchists were hunted out and eight anarchist leaders were arrested and convicted of murder. Six of these were executed and two given prison terms. It was not proved that any of them had committed the crime. They were convicted for the opinions they held.

Several years later, when John Peter Altgeld was elected governor of Illinois, he freed the two men who were still in prison, on the ground that their trial had been unfair.

Who threw the bomb in Haymarket Square is still not known. But executing and imprisoning the anarchist leaders did not bring the expected industrial peace. Only after that, the workers were more cautious. For a long time they had kept their meetings and their organizations secret—now they were more secret still.

And the employers had not succeeded in bringing labor peace when they acted so quickly in the Haymarket Square case. They could not really understand what the trouble was.

X

The Noble and Holy Order of the Knights of Labor

Seventeen years before the Haymarket riot, on December 9, 1869, nine tailors met in the hall of the American Hose Company in Philadelphia. They had belonged to the local Garment Cutters Association, but this organization had run out of funds and had been dissolved. The nine tailors now met to discuss forming a new association.

The leading spirit among the tailors was Uriah S. Stephens. A handsome man with a fine presence and a gift for making speeches, he had been educated as a Baptist minister, had tried schoolteaching, and only after that had learned the tailor's trade.

"We had better keep our new organization secret," Uriah Stephens told his companions. "There is not much chance for a workman if it is known that he belongs to a trade-union. Employers are making up black lists and refuse to employ any workman who belongs to a union. In a great many plants they lock out union members. And the courts don't give union men a fair trial. If we form an organization, we mustn't let it be known."

That was how the Noble and Holy Order of the Knights of Labor was begun. Before it was dissolved it was to last for about twenty years and have a membership of close to a million.

The philosophy of the Knights of Labor had a very religious tinge. Uriah Stephens, when he studied for the ministry, had been ingrained with the idea that labor is "noble and holy," and he believed that all men should live according to the Biblical injunction, "In the sweat of thy brow shalt thou eat bread."

The organization which was formed that day was to be of a new kind. It was to be founded on the principle of universal brotherhood. Every man who worked was to be admitted to it—the unskilled as well as the skilled, women as well as men, Negroes as well as white men. In their enthusiasm the tailors imagined that the Knights of Labor would not be confined to the United States. They would spread around the world.

"I can see ahead of me an organization that will cover the globe," Stephens said. "It will include men and women of every craft, creed, and color; it will cover every race worth saving."

As a matter of fact, membership in the Knights of Labor did not spread abroad. But in America all wage earners and all former wage earners were welcomed into its ranks. The only groups that were forbidden membership were lawyers, bankers, professional gamblers, stockbrokers, and persons connected with the sale of liquor.

"It gathers into one fold all branches of honorable toil," the constitution of the Knights of Labor announced.

For more than ten years the Knights of Labor were clothed in the deepest secrecy. In the years when the regular craft unions were going through desperate struggles, the membership of the Knights of Labor grew.

The very mystery of its rites and rituals made the Knights of Labor attractive to many people. It was like the Masons, the Elks, and the Knights of Pythias all joined together.

Terence V. Powderly, who was later to become head of the Knights of Labor, described how he was initiated:

A shopmate in the Cliff Locomotive Works of Scranton invited me to a 'labor lecture' to be given on the evening of September 6, 1876. I presented myself at the designated place, accompanied by my friend to the hall, and was mystified when we were ushered into a small room and told to wait a while. Soon after a man wearing a black gown and mask came out to question us. He seemed to be more satisfied with our answers than I was with his appearance, for I had no thought of joining a society of any kind that night.

Local Assembly No. 88 of the Knights of Labor was in session. My name had been proposed for membership, acted on favorably, and in the manner described I had been brought forward for initiation.

There was a great deal of drama in the proceedings of this secret society. The two chief officers were called "Grand Master" and "Venerable Sage." There were special handgrips and passwords, and notice of meetings was given by special code. No one ever spoke of the Knights of Labor by name. The society was called Five Stars. When a meeting was to be called you might find * * * * * written in chalk on sidewalk or fence, and with it cryptic symbols indicating the date, hour, and place of the meeting. Sometimes the * * * * * notice was printed in the newspaper.

In a short time the * * * * * had hundreds of thousands of members. Their slogan was "An injury to one is the concern of all." All the men and women who were members were bound to help each other. The carpenters were bound to come to the help of the plumbers, the machinists to the help of the tailors, etc.

As the organization grew, a list of concrete policies developed. They included the regular demands for better wages as well as the eight-hour day, the building of cooperatives, the abolition of child labor, the doing away with prison labor, contracts, and land and currency reform. * * * * * also demanded a graduated income tax and a federal bureau of labor statistics, government ownership of railroads and telegraph lines, and equal pay for men and women.

With their eyes set on such bright but distant goals membership in * * * * * grew faster and faster. But the secrecy which had been a protection in the beginning now proved a hindrance. For the Catholic Church, which objected to all secret societies, forbade its members to join this one. So the Knights of Labor came out into the open; the mysterious rites were given up. Then the Catholic Church withdrew its objections, and the membership grew faster than before.

In 1879 Uriah Stephens retired from the Knights of Labor, and Terence V. Powderly became Grand Master. He was only thirty at the time—the son of Irish Catholic parents.

As a boy Terence Powderly worked as a switch

tender in the railroad yards at Carbondale, Pennsylvania, but at seventeen he was apprenticed in the machinists' trade, and at twenty got a journeyman's job with the Delaware and Western in Scranton, Pennsylvania.

As he grew up he had a great many interests. Besides being labor mayor of Scranton, he studied law and practiced it, served as county health officer, and owned and managed a grocery store. Heading the Knights of Labor was perhaps the work at which he spent most time.

Those who knew him thought he did not look much like a labor leader. "Powderly was a slender man," a newspaper of the time asserts, "under average height with mild blue eyes behind glasses. He looks and behaves like a man of good breeding, accustomed to the usages of society.... All around him are strapping big fellows with hands and shoulders formidable to the eye, unpolished gems in the main. English novelists take men of Powderly's look for their poets, gondola scullers, philosophers and heroes crossed in love but no one ever drew such a looking man as the leader of a million of the horny-fisted sons of toil."

The new Grand Master was an eloquent orator and a good organizer, but he complained continually of being overworked.

"I am besieged from every quarter to lecture," he wrote. "I will not go. My throat is not strong enough to speak in public. . . . The Order has grown and is growing stronger every day, but I am not growing stronger and must have relief from unnecessary labor."

"I will talk at no picnics," he wrote on another occasion. "When I speak on the labor question, I want the individual attention of my hearers, and I want the attention for at least two hours, and in that two hours I can only epitomize. At a picnic, when the girls as well as the boys swill beer, I cannot talk at all. . . . If it comes to my ears that I am advertised to talk at picnics . . . I will prefer charges against the offenders for holding the executive up to ridicule."

Powderly had great dreams for the Order. "The Knights of Labor is higher and grander than party," he once said. "There is a nobler future before it than that which clings to its existence amidst partisan rancor and strife. . . ."

What was this future that he prophesied for the Knights? What were the principles that he discussed in the two-hour lectures, while the audience gave their "undivided attention"?

He did not believe in strikes. He thought they were too often unsuccessful and that they did not accomplish any permanent good. He knew that the Knights could not succeed in all their many objectives at once, so he pinned his faith to one of them—cooperation.

"It is to cooperation," he said in 1880, "that the eyes of the workingmen and workingwomen should be directed, upon cooperation their hopes should be centered. . . . There is no good reason why labor cannot, through cooperation, own and operate mines, factories, and railroads. . . ."

But labor had tried to help itself through a system of cooperatives before, and it had failed. It wanted better wages and it wanted to work shorter hours. In spite of Powderly's admonition, strike after strike broke out. The Grand Master, the visionary with his fine long speeches, somehow lost his influence. The Noble and Holy Order of the Knights of Labor, whose membership had risen to such triumphant heights, dwindled. By 1893 Powderly retired, and it was plain that the Order had declined to a point where it had little influence of any kind, though some of the Knights tried unsuccessfully to back their members for political offices.

But the failure and gradual disappearance of the Order was of no serious consequence. For by this time a new labor organization was coming to the fore.

XI

Samuel Gompers and the A. F. of L.

Samuel Gompers was twenty years old when he saw the police charge the crowd at the Tompkins Square riot in New York. From his vantage point in a cellarway he saw the people running and shouting, and heard the clatter of the horses' hoofs as the mounted police rode them down.

"In a certain way it's their own fault," he said to himself, watching the ragged and struggling unemployed. "They have made people think they are radicals and that they want to destroy the government."

In the years that followed, when he was working to build up the American Federation of Labor, Gompers took special pains never to appear to be a radical. He was, in fact, a conservative to the core.

He had come to this country with his mother and father when he was a boy of ten. They were of Dutch Jewish stock, and had been living in the East End of London where the father was a cigar maker. In New

York they found four rooms on the Lower East Side—
Gompers remembered afterward that they were a great
improvement over the quarters they had occupied in
London.

Though he was only ten, the boy was industrious and
strong, and it was decided that he should go to work
at once. Before long he was sitting with a dozen men in
a cigar-making shop, rolling brown leaves into cigars.

He liked it in the shop, and was proud to be treated
like a man. The cigar makers, many of them newly arrived immigrants, used to chip in together and pay one
of their number to read aloud. They had sent for a number of radical books that were printed in London, and
in this way the boy learned to discuss ideas and grew
interested in the labor movement.

As he grew older he talked with a great many Europeans who were socialists. He wrote in his autobiog-
raphy, *Seventy Years of Life and Labor:*

"In those days New York was the haven for over-
zealous soldiers in the European struggle for freedom. . . .
They were men of imagination, courage, ideals. They
sought their ends through revolution. . . ."

But Gompers himself, though he was interested in
them, never thought that revolutionary ideas were suitable to the American situation. America was a land of

promises where people could advance from the bottom to the top by hard work, he thought. "Revolutionists are not the type that readily adapt themselves to the customs of a new land," he wrote later. The American cigar makers could get the good conditions they wanted by building a strong organization. He would build up the Cigar Makers Union. Beyond that perhaps he could help to make the whole American labor movement practical.

Through the efforts of Gompers and his friends the cigar makers soon had one of the strongest of the skilled craftsmen's unions.

On December 8, 1886, they went to Columbus, Ohio, where members of other craft unions were holding a meeting. There were forty-two representatives there from twenty-five labor groups. Among them were iron molders, miners and mine workers, journeymen tailors, journeymen bakers, furniture workers, granite cutters, metalworkers, carpenters, and cigar makers.

These men organized themselves into what they called the American Federation of Labor, and elected Samuel Gompers their first president.

"There was much work, little pay, and very little honor," he wrote afterward. Nevertheless, he set about his work with characteristic vigor. Soon he had installed

74

himself in a little office which measured eight feet by ten. The Cigar Makers Union had provided it. Here a kitchen table served as a desk, some wooden boxes as chairs, and some tomato crates as files. Here he wrote endless letters in his own handwriting, planned speaking tours and organizing trips, and here he edited a labor newspaper, the *Trade Union Advocate*. Here also he issued union charters and collected union dues.

The American Federation of Labor was different from the Knights of Labor in almost every way. It had no idea of helping the whole mass of the American working people: it was merely an effort by members of the skilled crafts to help themselves. The members of the craft unions were joined together somewhat as the states are joined together in the federal government of the United States.

Gompers and his friends had seen unions fail in the past because they had not enough money to pay strike benefits over any very long period, or to weather a depression. Therefore, initiation fees and dues in the American Federation of Labor were high, and as the organization grew its business affairs were run as carefully as were the business affairs of the great corporations.

It took time and training to carry on the business affairs of the unions in this way. Gompers believed they could not depend on the spare time and energy of volunteers to get the work done. Therefore the officers and organizers were paid good salaries for the work they did. Some of the paid officials of the unions became skilled negotiators who could deal with representatives of the corporations in expert fashion. Those men in the big companies must have been surprised at their adroitness.

It is true that the paid representatives of the unions, who were trying to get all they could for labor, sometimes did not scruple to line their own pockets: they were labor racketeers. But after all it was an age of no great moral standards. The industrialists were trying to get all they could for themselves, too.

So the unions worked, surprising their employers with their cool-headed determination, surprising their own members perhaps. Not for them the distant dreams of land and currency reform and cooperatives. Nor were they willing to undertake political reform. They would "reward their friends and punish their enemies at the polls." That is, they would vote for the men who were favorable to labor. Beyond that they would not go into politics.

"We have no ultimate aims," one official of the American Federation of Labor told a Senate committee. "We are going on from day to day. We fight only for immediate objects—objects that can be realized in a few years."

Through thirty-eight years Samuel Gompers of the Cigar Makers Union was the moving spirit of the A. F. of L. Terence Powderly, with his spectacles and refined manners, had looked like a poet, but Samuel Gompers was a labor leader in looks as well as in fact. He was short, thickset, and sturdily built. ("The Gompers are built of oak," he used to say.) As a young man he wore a drooping walrus mustache with a tuft of hair on his chin. Later he was clean-shaven, but he always had thick, unruly hair—black at first, turning later to a mop of white. His dark eyes snapped behind glasses, and his voice had a rich resonance as he boomed out speeches in city after city.

He seemed never to be tired. He traveled back and forth across the country talking to industrialists ("He appears quite a gentleman," they said patronizingly) or to meetings of workingmen ("I have not risen from the ranks, I am proud to be in the ranks," he said). He was a man of tremendous gusto, who liked to smoke cigars, drink beer, go to music halls, and walk on the boardwalk at Atlantic City. But he also liked to wear a Prince Albert coat and to be accepted by the captains of industry.

This was the man who was to shape the policy of American organized labor for nearly forty years.

XII

Detectives and Armed Guards

Before the end of the nineteenth century the corporations of America had grown to enormous proportions. Oil, steel, coal, sugar—the men who controlled those corporations were powerful as kings, and richer than any foreign potentates. But the unions had also grown powerful now. They were well organized and strong, with dues that came pouring into their treasuries from thousands of members. It was not strange that there should be a collision between these two great forces, or that the shock of that collision should be felt throughout the country.

It started in July, 1892, when the Carnegie Steel Company ignored the contract it had made with the Amalgamated Association of Iron, Steel and Tin Workers.

Andrew Carnegie was the head of the steel company and he was apparently sympathetic to labor. But Carnegie was at his castle in Scotland that summer. Henry

Clay Frick was general manager of the Carnegie Steel Company. He hated organized labor and was determined to break the unions.

On July 6, therefore, he announced to the workers at the steel plant at Homestead, Pennsylvania, that there would be a cut in wages, although the union's contract had not expired. The union objected. Frick closed down the plant and announced that he would rehire only those men who were willing to work at the lower wage. He had anticipated trouble and had already built a tall fence around the plant. The fence was topped with barbed wire, and pierced with holes suitable for rifle barrels.

Now, since the union men would not come back to work for the wages he offered, Frick arranged to hire strikebreakers to do their jobs. And since he knew that the strikebreakers would have difficulty in getting through the picket lines which the union men threw around the plant, he hired armed guards from the Pinkerton Detective Agency to protect them.

The Pinkerton men started for Homestead under cover of the dark: two barges carried them up the river. They were armed with Winchester rifles. At about four o'clock in the morning they reached Homestead and prepared to land.

But the strikers had been notified of their coming.

Men, women, and children were waiting along the shore. As the first of the armed guards walked down the gangplank a shot rang out. It is not known whether that first shot was fired by a union man or by a Pinkerton man. But now the Pinkertons opened fire into the crowd and several of the workers were hit.

The fighting lasted thirteen hours. After a while the Pinkerton men were driven back to the river and took refuge in their barges. Then the strikers poured oil on the river water and set fire to it. So finally the Pinkerton men ran up a white flag and surrendered. Union leaders tried to give them a safe-conduct to the railroad station, as they ran through a shower of stones.

Now all was quiet at Homestead for several days, the strike held, the furnaces were cold. Then on July 12 the Pennsylvania state militia marched in, sent by the governor to protect the steel plant. Then the company started hiring strikebreakers again under military protection, and so, finally, the strike was broken. The men could do nothing in the face of the militia's guns.

The militia continued its vigil at Homestead, and the company went on hiring strikebreakers. By November it was useless for the union to hold out any longer, and the strike was declared over. The steelworkers' union had been completely smashed. It was not reorganized effectively again for nearly forty years. The steel company had succeeded in its efforts by hiring armed guards and by the use of the state militia, but the country as a whole was not sure what these weapons might mean in the industrial warfare that threatened the United States.

Andrew Carnegie, strangely enough, expressed himself as being in sympathy with the striking men. He wrote: "To expect that one dependent upon his daily wage for the necessaries of life will stand by peacefully and see a new man employed in his stead is to expect too much." And he wrote to his friend Sir William Gladstone, the British statesman, "The pain I suffer increases daily. The Works are not worth one drop of human blood. I wish they had been sunk."

But Carnegie, vacationing at Skibo Castle in Scotland, must have known what Frick's ideas were. And he himself had appointed Frick.

The newspapers almost all backed the steel company. Had they not the right to provide protection for whomsoever they chose to employ? the newspaper editors asked. If the Homestead workers did not like the wages offered them, let them go to work elsewhere.

There were heated discussions about the Homestead Strike in Congress. Some members thought the armed guards the steel company had hired constituted a paid army, and that the workers had a right to resist this army to protect their jobs and their homes. But other members thought that such ideas as this were absurd and that the steel company had a perfect right to do what they had done.

In the years after the Homestead Strike the Carnegie Steel Company prospered as it had never done before. Other industrialists watched it with envy and considered using weapons similar to those the steel company had used when industrial warfare threatened.

But hiring armed guards was expensive, and state governors were not always ready to call out the militia. The industrialists began to look for other ways of settling wage disputes. They turned to the courts, and discovered the injunction.

XIII

An Injunction Settles a Strike

An injunction is a court order which a judge may issue at his own discretion. It may forbid picketing, making speeches, holding meetings, distributing leaflets, or doing a dozen other things. Anyone who disobeys an injunction may be held in "contempt of court" and punished for such disobedience without a jury trial. The injunction is a very powerful weapon indeed, as Americans were soon to find out. It was effectively used when the workers of the Pullman Palace Car Company went out on strike in 1894.

The scene of the action was the town of Pullman in Illinois. That town is part of the city of Chicago now, but it was originally a separate town owned and managed by the Pullman Company. George Pullman, head of the company, spoke of it as a "model" town, and pointed with pride to the little brick houses that were grouped around grassy squares. Here lived the employees of the factories, workshops, and mills, and the company owned every stick and stone in the place—the houses, the school, the church, the library, the grocery store—all these belonged to the Pullman Company. The Pullman Company also owned and operated all the utilities in the town—the water, gas and electricity, and also the garbage disposal.

The employees paid the company what they owed for rent and services each payday. The amount each man owed was deducted from his pay envelope.

The men knew that the rents they paid for their houses were generally 25 per cent higher than they would have paid for similar houses in neighboring communities. Utilities and food in the company store were correspondingly high. But there was nothing they could do about it. If they worked for the Pullman Company, they had to live there.

Then a business depression struck the country, and the Pullman Palace Car Company found its orders falling off. The company had to find some way of cutting corners, though it did not wish to cut the 8 per cent dividend it paid to stockholders. Therefore, it laid off 5,800 employees, and announced that it would cut the wages of those men who remained on the pay roll by about 30 per cent. No provision was made for lowering rents, however, and charges for services and food at the company stores were as high as ever.

Now the men found the money in their pay envelopes dwindling. They received generally somewhere between one dollar and six dollars for two weeks, after their debts to the company had been paid. One man got fifty cents.

The men decided to hold a meeting to discuss what could be done. Since there was no hall in the town of Pullman where they were allowed to meet, they went to a neighboring town. They decided that they would send a committee to talk things over with Mr. Pullman.

Mr. Pullman said there was nothing he could do about the matter. Almost immediately afterward three men who were members of the committee were notified that they were discharged.

So 2,500 workers at the Pullman Company went on strike. By noon next day 800 more walked out. The company posted a notice on its gate announcing that the plant would be shut indefinitely.

The American Railway Union was an organization of railway employees of which Eugene V. Debs was head, and the Pullman strikers now appealed to this union for help.

Debs was thirty-nine years old at the time of the Pullman Strike, tall, gaunt, and nearly bald. He was a very gentle and idealistic person. Clarence Darrow, the well-known lawyer, said of him: "There may have lived some time, somewhere, a kindlier, gentler, more generous man than Eugene Debs, but I have not known him."

Debs was greatly opposed to any kind of violence. He advised the strikers to see Mr. Pullman again and try to arbitrate. But Mr. Pullman said there was "nothing to arbitrate." So the American Railway Union agreed to help the Pullman men.

On June 21, 1894, they met in convention and gave Mr. Pullman an ultimatum. Unless he agreed within four days to negotiate a settlement with the employees, a strike would be ordered. Mr. Pullman again said there was "nothing to arbitrate."

Then on every railroad that ran into Chicago there was a boycott of the Pullman Palace cars. Railroad men who were members of the American Railway Union refused to inspect, switch, or haul any Pullman cars. This was a very serious matter for Pullman. His company was a member of a powerful organization called the General Managers Association, which was a group of railroad executives. This organization stood behind Pullman now.

The General Managers Association knew what to do. They ordered that cars carrying mail be attached to the Pullman cars. Then, if a switchman cut a Pullman car from the track, he also cut off a mail car—he was interfering with the United States mail. In addition to this, they ordered that all men who refused to handle Pullman cars be discharged.

That resulted in a general strike on the railroads.

Things happened quickly after that. The General Managers Association called on the United States marshal at Chicago for special deputies to prevent obstruction of mails and to protect their property. The Attorney General of the United States authorized the hiring of 3,600 deputies who were armed and paid by the railroads. The bill amounted to $400,000.

It was clear that violence might result, and John Peter Altgeld, governor of Illinois, held the militia in readiness. But the Managers Association would not wait. Richard B. Olney, who was Attorney General, charged the union with conspiracy to restrain transportation and obstruct the United States mail. And forthwith Judge Peter S. Grosscup issued an injunction against Debs and sixteen other union officials restraining them "from in any way or manner interfering with, hindering, obstructing, or stopping" any of the business of the railroads entering Chicago or any trains carrying United States mail or engaging in interstate commerce.

Then Olney prevailed on President Cleveland to send

federal troops to enforce the injunction. Four companies of the 15th Infantry were soon patrolling the railroad yards.

Governor Altgeld telegraphed President Cleveland protesting the arrival of the federal troops. He said, "If any assistance is needed the state stands ready to furnish a hundred men for every one man required, and stands ready to do so at a moment's notice."

The injunction and the presence of the federal troops seemed to the men an infringement of their rights as citizens. If an employer could prevail on the government to issue an injunction and enforce it with troops, what chance had they to organize? they asked.

Debs called a convention which was scheduled to meet in Chicago, July 12, 1894, for the purpose of discussing a sympathy strike throughout the United States. Since this was construed as disobedience to the court's order, he was imprisoned, together with three other Railway Union officials.

So the Pullman Company and the General Managers Association had their way. The strikers, with their leaders in jail, were disillusioned, disheartened, and despondent. The railroad strike was called off August 5, 1894, and the men at Pullman went back to work on September 6 of that year.

There was a great deal of discussion about the Pullman Strike in all the newspapers after that. What did the events at Pullman mean to the United States? Many objected to what they called "government by injunction" and thought that Cleveland's use of the troops had not been justified.

President Theodore Roosevelt said some time later:

"It is all wrong to use the injunction to prevent the entirely proper and legitimate actions of labor organizations in their struggle for industrial betterment, or under the guise of protecting property right unwarrantably to invade the fundamental rights of the individual. It is futile to concede, as we all do, the right and necessity of organized effort on the part of wage earners and yet by injunctive process to forbid peaceable action to accomplish the lawful objects for which they are organized and upon which their success depends."

Still, in Theodore Roosevelt's time no better way of settling labor disputes had been found.

XIV

Progress in T. R.'s Time

"Capital must learn to get along with labor." This statement, surprising enough in its time, was printed in the Springfield *Republican* in 1902. Learning to "get along with labor" was not easy for capital. Theodore Roosevelt's action in the strike of the anthracite coal miners that same year showed an attitude that was new.

Conditions in the coal mines had been turbulent since their beginning, and the efforts of the miners to improve their lot had never been successful. The "Long Strike" of 1874-1875 had resulted in ignominious defeat for them: they had been so thoroughly beaten and discouraged that they had not tried to organize again for many years. Then, because the men were grossly underpaid, because the work of the mines was dangerous with its cave-ins and poison gases, and because of layoffs bringing hunger whenever the bosses decided to cut down the working force—because of all these things, the miners sought

again and again to organize. In 1902 they were successful, for the coal miners signed up by the thousands.

The United Mine Workers called a strike in the bituminous coal mines of Pennsylvania, Ohio, Indiana, and
Michigan in that same year. They won recognition of
the union and some agreement with regard to hours and
wages. Then they moved over into the anthracite coal
fields of Pennsylvania.

There were nine "hard-coal" counties in Pennsylvania.
Coal mining was such an all-pervading industry in these
counties that the people who lived there spoke of the
place as a separate entity. They called it "Anthracite."

The little towns in Anthracite where the miners lived
were covered with black dirt from the mines. The dirt
got ingrained in the people's skin so that they nearly all
had a kind of grayish complexion. Nothing much grew
in the black soil—it was covered with coal dust and
poisoned with fumes from the mines. At the mine entrances the small, unpainted houses of the miners were
set along unpaved streets. They belonged, not to the
miners themselves, but to the company. Samuel Gompers
said of the miners that "they were brought into the world
by the company doctor, lived in a company house or
hut, were nurtured by the company store . . . and laid
away in the company graveyard."

Tall structures, called breakers, overshadowed the houses of these towns. At the top of these, heavy machines broke the big chunks of coal into pieces. Then the broken pieces came pouring down zigzag chutes from the top of the structure so that the slate could be picked out of the coal as it moved along. Little boys, most of them not more than nine or ten years old, stood beside the chutes to pick out the slate with their fingers. It is hard to distinguish between slate and coal. They had to put their faces down close to see. The children started at seven in the morning and worked until six at night, with an hour for lunch.

There was a law in Pennsylvania forbidding the employment of children in the mining industry, but this was generally ignored.

Some of the men who went down in the elevators to work in the dangerous pockets of the coal strata were Irish and Welsh who had emigrated much earlier, but the vast majority were newly arrived immigrants: they were Hungarians, Poles, Slovaks, and Italians.

The strike in the anthracite coal mines began on May 9, 1902. The operators were well prepared for it. They had brought 3,000 iron and coal police into the area, as well as 1,000 other police deputies. The company started at once to bring in strikebreakers, but had difficulty in securing them, for most men do not know how to mine coal, and few will even try to do it if they can find any other jobs.

The men watched all these newcomers moving about in their towns and going into the mines, but took no action. There was no violence; they simply refused to mine coal until they had been listened to.

So week followed week. Now they had been on strike two months, now three, now four. Once a week they went to union headquarters to get meager strike benefits so that their wives could buy food. When the company refused to sell them coal to heat their houses, as it had formerly done, their children went with baskets to pick bits of coal from the slag heaps. They ran away nimbly if police came after them.

All this time there was no weakening in the union ranks, and there was no violence. The high morale of the miners may be attributed in very large measure to one man—John Mitchell, president of the United Mine Workers, whom the men admired and loved. His statue may still be seen in the public square in Scranton.

John Mitchell was slight in build but wiry. He had brown eyes and an olive complexion so that he might have been mistaken for an Italian. But Mitchell's disposition was much more Anglo-Saxon than it was Latin.

He was quiet and almost diffident, willing to listen to both sides of a question, conciliatory. He knew how to get on with men of every nationality.

Mitchell had worked in the mines himself as a boy of twelve. The men had elected him their president when he was only twenty-eight. Like many another labor leader, he hated strikes. When matters came to a head in the anthracite coal fields he proposed arbitration. The National Civic Federation was a newly constituted body of representative leaders in both labor and industry. "Let the National Civic Federation appoint a committee of five," Mitchell said. "Or let them make a committee composed of Archbishop Ireland, Bishop Potter, and any third person they choose." And he continued:

"If they decide that the average annual wages received by the anthracite miners are sufficient to enable them to live, maintain, and educate their families in a manner consistent with American citizenship, we agree to withdraw our claims to higher wages and more equitable conditions of employment, providing that the anthracite mine operators agree to comply with any recommendations the above committee may make affecting the earnings and conditions of labor of their employees."

It seemed like a reasonable suggestion. But the spokesman for the mine operators replied to it, saying, "Anthracite mining is a business and not a religious, sentimental, or academic proposition."

So the strike dragged on. As the cold winter months approached, fewer and fewer carloads of coal were brought out of the mining regions. Sympathy was with the miners in the country as a whole, but industry depended largely on steam boilers fired with coal, and domestic heating was done almost entirely by coal: America at that time could not get on unless some way was found to mine its coal.

President Theodore Roosevelt was not a man to sit idly by in this time of crisis. He called for a meeting of operators and union representatives at Washington, D. C. It was October 3 and the cold of winter was close at hand.

At this meeting John Mitchell again made his proposal that an impartial committee be appointed to arbitrate. And again the spokesman for the operators derided the proposal and rebuked the President for listening to the miners. He said that they were "fomenters of anarchy" and that they had shown "insolent defiance of the law."

Theodore Roosevelt was not a man of great patience; he was angry now. He let it be known that he had made a plan to send the United States troops into the mining regions. If the operators refused to arbitrate with the union, he would dispossess them, and the government would operate the mines.

President Cleveland had ordered out the troops in 1894 at the time of the Pullman Strike, and by this means he had brought the dissension to an end and broken the union. But Theodore Roosevelt planned to send troops to the Pennsylvania coal mines for a very different purpose. Now he was saying to the operators, "There are two sides to this question." He was using pressure to have them come to terms.

When Theodore Roosevelt threatened to use the great power of his office in this way, the operators quickly agreed that they would accept the terms of an arbitration commission if he would appoint one. The commission made its recommendations and the miners accepted them. All this is remembered today because now, for the first time, the claims of labor were being listened to in high places.

The coal strike of 1902 has been called the "most important single event in labor history." One historian writes of it ". . . for the first time a labor organization tied up for months a strategic industry and caused widespread suffering and discomfort to the public without being condemned as a revolutionary menace to the existing social order calling for suppression by the government."

The liberal attitude of the public toward the United Mine Workers was only one evidence of a new spirit that was growing in America at the turn of the century. In many states child labor laws were being passed, as well as laws which regulated the work of women. The first minimum wage law went into effect in Massachusetts in 1912, and eight other states passed similar statutes in the following years. Workmen's compensation laws, which provided that if a man was hurt or killed at his work the state would provide compensation, were also passed in many states. They were a great step forward, for besides the fact that they were humanitarian, they acknowledged that the state should bear the responsibility for an injury and not the workman who sustained it.

Taken all together, then, despite the efforts of some reactionary industrialists, it was an era of understanding and of hope that was altogether new in the history of labor. To many it appeared that industrial peace and justice might be just over the horizon.

And then, in 1914, World War I was declared.

XV

"One Big Union"

Before America became involved in World War I, however, a new organization called the Industrial Workers of the World, or I. W. W., came sweeping across the country. It started in Chicago.

Chicago was the city to which migratory workers drifted from every part of the continent at the beginning of the twentieth century. Here the streets swarmed with men looking for work or resting up between jobs. Here were assembled harvest hands and fruit pickers, loggers and lake seamen, road builders and men who laid railroad tracks. They stood around in little knots at the street corners and crowded into the cheap restaurants and dance halls.

In prosperous times as many as a million men a year came to Chicago and shipped out of there again. They came on foot, or stealing rides on the freight cars: most of them had no money to pay for transportation.

There was a big meeting hall on Madison Street in Chicago then, and it was crowded with people day and night. There were blackboards along the walls of that hall where jobs were listed—jobs in the harvest fields, jobs in the mines and in the orchards, jobs picking apples or cherries or hops, all in their season. Men coming into the hall to search those blackboards had to pass through a door where a big red emblem was painted. It was the emblem of the I. W. W.—the Industrial Workers of the World.

Mass meetings were held at night in the hall on Madison Street under the hot gaslights. The place was hardly big enough to hold all the men who crowded into those meetings. Sometimes, when the crowds overflowed the hall, meetings were called outside. Then the street was packed so thick with men that horses and wagons could not get through.

For Chicago before World War I was the center for the I. W. W.'s—the "wobblies" people called them out West. The history of that organization is a colorful one.

"Big Bill" Haywood was the chief organizer of the I. W. W. The men knew him as a stoop-shouldered, one-eyed giant of a man who was not averse to violence. He had been a lumberman, a cowhand, and a miner in the copper, silver, and lead mines of Colorado, Minnesota, and Nevada. He was one of the chief officers of the Western Federation of Miners, and in that capacity he was continually urging the miners to meet violence with sabotage—to flood and dynamite the mines when the owners machine-gunned the miners' meetings, to meet strikebreakers and Pinkerton detectives with clubs and bullets.

But Haywood soon realized that they could not accomplish much in a struggle with the entrenched power of the mine owners. If the miners could join with workers of other industries and have "one big union" they would have more strength, he said. The idea grew as he talked with others about it. It was to be "one big union, one big strike." When they heard that a meeting of radical workers was to be held in Chicago in 1905, the western miners decided that this was a chance to get their "one big union" started. So they sent five delegates to Chicago.

There were all sorts of people at the meeting in Chicago. Daniel De Leon, the brilliant socialist orator, was there, and the gentle idealist, Eugene Debs. There, too, were Father T. J. Hagerty, a black-bearded Catholic priest who was editor of a labor newspaper, and the German leader of the United Brewery Workers. A fiery old lady with curly white hair and gray eyes took part in every session: everybody seemed to know her. They called her "Mother Jones." "Big Bill" Haywood was the most vital of all the delegates at Chicago. Under his leadership the Industrial Workers of the World grew out of the Chicago meeting.

When Samuel Gompers heard of the meeting at Chicago he was filled with scorn. Such a strange collection of people would never hang together, he said. And in the long run Gompers turned out to be right.

The ideas on which the I. W. W. was based were very different from those of the A. F. of L. For the A. F. of L. believed in the capitalist system. They believed that one group of people, those who had capital to invest, ought to own the factories, the fields, and the mines, together with the machinery that would make them productive, while another group contributed their labor and worked for wages. In this way they believed that America would prosper. The only reason labor must organize, they held, was that united they could insure good working conditions, hours of work that were not too long, and good pay. "A fair day's work for a fair day's pay," was their slogan.

Bill Haywood and the members of the I. W. W. were directly opposed to the A. F. of L. ideas. They could see no good whatever in the capitalist system, for they held that the capitalist and the worker had nothing in common. The wage system ought to be done away with, they said: the workers themselves ought to own and run the factories and mines. They ought to be the owners of all the wealth in the country.

The I. W. W. leaders were not dreamers, but essentially practical in making their plans. There were thirteen major industries in the United States, they pointed out. If the workers in each of these could be organized, it would be possible to call them all out on strike at once. "One big union, one big strike" would mean that the workers could take control. This was a philosophy of revolution.

The doctrines discussed at the 1905 Chicago meeting were inflammable. The fire of them spread across the country. In lumber camps and in the shacks where the fruit pickers and harvest hands slept, the revolutionary ideas were talked about. They were discussed in the barren little towns at mine entrances, and by the foreign-born who worked in the eastern textile mills. To unskilled workers who were not eligible to join the ranks of organized labor, the ideas of the I. W. W. were especially appealing.

For the I. W. W. was not exclusive. The new organization welcomed everyone to its ranks. It took in the unskilled as well as the skilled, the foreign-born, the

Negroes, and the women who were being employed in larger and larger numbers. Those groups had been excluded by the A. F. of L.

The A. F. of L. selected its members according to their crafts—all the plumbers were in one union, all the carpenters in another, all the electricians in a third. But the I. W. W. did not confine itself to skilled craftsmen: they wanted everyone in an industry to join together. That meant that all the workers in the steel mills, skilled or unskilled, were to be in one union, all those in the textile industry in another, and so on. High and low, skilled and unskilled, all were to be joined together. The "one big union" was not to be made up of skilled craftsmen: it was to be an organization of industrial unions. This same idea was to be carried out later by the C. I. O.

"We are going down into the gutter to get at the mass of workers and bring them up to a decent plane of living," Bill Haywood wrote enthusiastically.

So the I. W. W. set to work. They wrote songs that were sung at mass meetings and on picket lines and around the evening campfires when work in the orchards or harvest fields was done. The songs were badly rhymed, but they were full of vitality and sung with lusty vigor.

Besides stirring up enthusiasm in this way, the I. W.

W. leaders tried to do a large job of education. They wanted to explain to the people the principles on which they worked. That meant making speeches—hundreds of street-corner speeches in little towns and big. So they were soon mounting soapboxes at the street corners to talk to the crowds.

It did not take the town authorities in most places long to object to this speechmaking. When the speakers refused to stop talking, the authorities seized them and locked them up. But this measure was not very successful, for the jails were not big enough to hold all the speechmakers: as soon as the town authorities arrested one of them a dozen others appeared and went on talking. The Constitution had guaranteed freedom of speech, the I. W. W. pointed out. It was all very perplexing. But meantime "civil rights speeches," as they came to be called, were echoing across the country.

The new organization was as good at organizing strikes as it was at singing and speechmaking. There were I. W. W. strikes in the canneries of the Northwest; in the Midwestern steel and meat-packing plants; among the window cleaners and transportation workers in the East. Their organizers did not even wait for the workers in an industry to join the organization. They went to help any group of unorganized or unskilled workers who needed them.

That was the situation in Lawrence, Massachusetts, in 1912, where, without warning, the American Woolen Company cut the wages of the thirty thousand foreign-born textile workers in their factories. The men and women had been getting less than $9.00 a week already, and when they opened their pay envelopes and found that they had still less than this, they had left their machines and gone pouring out into the streets. They had no union, and in fact very little understanding of their rights, but they knew they could not live on the money they received. The I. W. W. sent two men, Joseph Ettor and Arturo Giovannitti, to help organize the strike in Lawrence.

Soon picket lines were set up, soup kitchens started, and funds collected from workers in other industries. Pamphlets and handbills were also distributed, and since most of the workers could not read English, they were printed in Russian, Lithuanian, Polish, and Italian.

The story of the Lawrence strike has been told often. Ettor and Giovannitti were accused of planting dynamite and imprisoned. But they were later exonerated by the court and released.

As the weeks wore on it was decided to send the

children of the strikers to be taken care of in other communities. When they were lined up in the railroad station ready to leave, the police jostled them and treated them so roughly that public opinion was completely turned in the direction of the strikers. The strike was settled in favor of the workers not long after that.

There were other strikes in other New England textile mills which the I. W. W. leaders managed to carry to a successful conclusion. And the membership of the organization grew until at one time it reached about sixty thousand. But though their energy and activity kept adding to the I. W. W. membership lists, the names kept dropping off again. "Wobblies" never stayed long in one place and were not accustomed to holding very long to any one thing.

So the I. W. W. leaders worked and talked and organized, and their revolutionary ideas might in the end have had some influence on the trend of American industrial life. But then World War I broke out and, though the I. W. W. continued to exist, its influence disappeared.

For "Big Bill" Haywood, who was still their leader, announced that the I. W. W. would not support the American government in the war. He announced that the members of his organization would evade the draft and would not cooperate in any way in the war effort.

"We as members of the industrial army will refuse to fight for any purpose except for the realization of industrial freedom," Bill Haywood said.

As a result of this stand Bill Haywood and ninety-four other I. W. W. leaders were convicted and sentenced to jail terms up to twenty years. Haywood afterward escaped and fled to Russia, where he died.

A leaderless organization now had little chance of exerting much influence. Perhaps the influence of the I. W. W. would not have amounted to much anyhow for America had changed since Haywood first had talked of "one big union." Machinery was taking the place of migratory labor in many harvest fields and orchards now. There was no need of the great hosts of men that had moved up and down and back and forth across the continent. When the soldiers came back from the war, most of them stayed in settled communities: many went back and forth to work in automobiles. American life was different from the way it had been before the war.

Just as the rank-and-file membership was changed by World War I, so its leadership was changed. Besides the many leaders who were now in prison, there were many others who deserted to join the Communist party.

So the workingmen of the postwar age never learned

the stirring old I. W. W. songs, and though there were strikes they were not helped by I. W. W. organizers. The I. W. W. still existed but few people paid any attention to it.

Why, then, remember it at all? Did its existence make any difference in the final summing up of the labor story?

It seems clear that the appearance and the virtual disappearance of the I. W. W. did have some influence. Its existence and its lack of success seem to prove that though labor might go through struggles and misery in its progress toward peace and justice, revolution was not in the American temper. America had been born of political revolution, but when it came to labor relations she was searching for a way of peace.

That testing of the American philosophy was a negative contribution, but the I. W. W. had also positive contributions to make, for the I. W. W. directed the attention of labor leaders to the great mass of unskilled laborers whose work was also needed in America. And the I. W. W. showed the people that their strength lay in using the contributions of the foreign-born, of the Negro workers, and the women workers, and of all who came with their various gifts to make their contribution to America. There was a suspicion in many places that

the old exclusive craft unions of the A. F. of L. were becoming outmoded. Nevertheless, the A. F. of L. continued in its exclusive way for nearly a quarter of a
century.

XVI

"This Is Labor's War"

World War I nearly destroyed the I. W. W. when that organization refused to support it. But it gave Samuel Gompers and the A. F. of L. a great push forward. "This is labor's war," Gompers said, pledging that labor would cooperate with the government. The great mass of American workingmen stood behind Gompers.

It is true that organized labor had made great advances in America in the years before the country went to war. In 1914 Congress had passed the Clayton Act, and news of its passage had been hailed with rejoicing, for it had stated clearly that labor unions might not be prosecuted under the antitrust laws. "The Clayton Act is labor's Magna Carta," Gompers had said. Certainly it was a great step forward. Ever since the Philadelphia cordwainers had been brought to court for forming a union back in 1806 the courts had blocked the progress of the unions. They had issued injunctions against them, and been more than willing to prosecute them under the anti-trust laws. Such actions by the courts had been real blocks to labor's progress. Now, however, the Clayton Act stated clearly that labor organizations "created for the purpose of mutual help and not conducted for profit were to be exempted from prosecution under the anti-trust laws." And they maintained further that a peaceable strike or boycott was not to be considered a violation of the law. Besides all this, the act definitely forbade any court to grant an injunction against labor in any dispute "concerning the terms or conditions of employment, unless necessary to prevent irreparable injury to property."

That last provision certainly provided a loophole—for who was to decide when damage to property was irreparable? But the labor leaders in 1914 ignored the possible loopholes and rejoiced that the Clayton Act had been passed.

They were enthusiastic now also because they had a President in the White House who was sensitive to their needs and rights. In his inaugural address the austere and learned Woodrow Wilson, whom the politicians liked to call "The Schoolmaster," proclaimed his "New Freedom." In this new freedom, he said, measures should be taken not only to safeguard the workers' lives but to improve the conditions under which they lived and worked and to provide "rational and tolerable" hours of labor. As if these things were not enough, he added another: workmen should have "freedom to act in their own interest," he said.

That meant, of course, that they had a right to organize.

Encouraged by such statements as these, labor lost no time in building up its strength. Organizers were soon in every mill, mine, and factory. Membership in existing unions increased, and new unions sprang up everywhere. The United Mine Workers became the strongest union in the country and had the largest membership. But the newly organized building-trade unions, the carpenters, painters, masons, and bricklayers, were powerful, too—they built their membership up to 300,000. And in the eastern cities the garment workers formed enthusiastic unions with fresh ideas and new ways of doing things.

The passage of the Clayton Act and Woodrow Wilson's formulation of the New Freedom were not the only encouraging occurrences. In the years before World War I labor had long objected to the arrival of unlimited numbers of the foreign-born because they believed they glutted the labor market. Now Congress passed a literacy test for immigrants which limited to some extent the numbers of those who were admitted to America.

And labor had objected to the conditions under which seamen worked in the United States merchant ships. But in 1915 the La Follette Seamen's Act was passed: it regulated the seamen's pay, their working conditions, and the number of hours they worked.

The number of hours a man should be required to work had been a bone of contention for many years. But now the Adamson Act established an eight-hour day on the railroads, and workingmen were hopeful that the standard the government set for the railroads might be carried over into other industries.

So in many ways the prospect for labor seemed fair in the years before World War I. "We are no longer in the season of planting: we are in harvest time," Samuel Gompers said. He had no way of seeing what stormy days still lay ahead.

Indeed, it seems that Samuel Gompers with his heavy-set jaw and his bushy gray hair was a little too exuberant, for the great mass-production industries were not yet organized. There were no unions in the steel mills, where the Poles, Russians, and Italians were working in the glaring lights of the blast furnaces for as much as twelve hours a day. Nor were the men organized in the factories that turned out farm machinery and automobiles. And there was no union in the big meat-packing industry. The corporations were still hostile to labor no matter what the government might say. There were still low wages and there were still long hours, for 90 per cent of the American workingmen were unorganized.

Nevertheless, organized or not, American workingmen remembered that they were citizens when America went to war. They held the interests of their country above their own separate interests.

"Wrapped up with the safety of this Republic are ideals of democracy," one union leader wrote, "a heritage which the masses of the people received from our forefathers, who fought that liberty might live in this country—a heritage that is to be maintained and handed down to each generation with undiminished power and usefulness."

In proof of the sincerity of their attitude a group of representatives of seventy-nine labor unions and of the Railway Brotherhoods held a meeting March 1, 1917. Here they formulated a statement, "America's Labor Position in Peace and in War."

"America shall have labor's full support in the war," the statement pledged. "In return she will expect the

United States to place orders for government contracts through the medium of the unions, and to give representation to the unions on all the boards that deal with national defense."

The war started a month later, and the ships began carrying American boys across the ocean to fight in France. But for every soldier that was sent to fight, the work of many men was needed to supply him with munitions, food, and uniforms. One historian has estimated that it took the work of as many as twenty men to give one soldier the supplies which he needed. Workers were needed also in the shipyards, for it took an enormous fleet of hastily built wooden vessels to carry the army abroad.

Prices always rise during wartime. Food, cloth, leather, metal, lumber, and fuel—all are needed for the army, and all, therefore, become scarce at home. Scarce products quickly become expensive ones.

The United States was no exception to the rule. The men and women in mills, mines, and factories saw the price of all the articles they bought rising, but they saw also that the amount of money in the pay envelopes would not buy so much: their wages had remained constant, but what are called their "real wages" had been reduced. The workers feared the poverty that would result from a reduction in their real wages: in many places they went on strike.

Soon the number of strikes increased. It was estimated that there were 4,450 strikes before the end of 1917. Nearly a million workers were involved in them.

This was a very dangerous situation, for not only did the strikes cause suffering to the men involved, but the work stoppage cut down the supplies that were needed to carry on the war. The soldiers could not fight without munitions, food, and uniforms. They could not even be taken to the fighting zone without ships. The government must act.

In this critical situation Woodrow Wilson decided to get the advice of both management and labor, and he called five representatives of each of these groups to a meeting in Washington. He also invited two representatives of the general public to the meeting. One of these was former President Taft.

What could these men, sitting around a great table in their conference room in Washington, do while the soldiers waited for the shoes and uniforms the factories had stopped turning out, the food that needed to be processed and packed, the guns and the bullets?

The representatives that Woodrow Wilson had called to Washington were soon organized into the National

War Labor Board. After brief discussion they succeeded in making plans to keep the factory wheels running and the mines and mills operating. They announced that it was necessary for both management and labor to make concessions, and these were made generously, without much delay.

First of all, the representatives of labor pledged that there would be no more strikes for the duration of the war. It is easy to understand with what relief the country heard of this agreement.

But before they could agree that there should be no strikes, labor had certain requirements to ask on her side, and these also were granted. Gompers and those with him asked that the government accept "the right of all workers, including common laborers, to a living wage . . . which will insure the subsistence of the worker and his family in health and reasonable comfort." Such a wage was now agreed upon in all government contracts. Beyond this Gompers had further requirements to make, and these, too, were agreed to. It was acknowledged and clearly stated that labor had a right to organize and to bargain collectively. All existing labor agreements were now upheld, and it was agreed that the eight-hour day should prevail as nearly as possible in all places where government work was carried on. Women were being employed in larger and larger numbers in the factories, now that so many men had gone to the front —and it was agreed that they should receive equal pay with men if they did equal work. This not only benefited the women, who in many instances were supporting families, but it kept up the wage standard for all workers.

Woodrow Wilson with the grave responsibilities of war resting on his slight shoulders listened to all these agreements and these concessions with satisfaction. He had seen the country's war effort threatened by a blockage of the country's industrial production. He had found a way to deal with that threat. There were many other problems and many tragedies to face, but this one, at least, he had found a way to deal with. He gave credit for the success of the undertaking to Samuel Gompers. He said: "I want to express my admiration of his patriotic courage, his large vision, and his statesmanlike sense of what had to be done."

XVII

The Steel Companies Talk of Communism

In January, 1919, President Wilson sailed for Paris to attend the Peace Conference. The armistice had been signed the week before: the war was over. Now on every vessel the boys were coming home. Soon in every part of America they were taking off their uniforms, putting on unaccustomed civilian clothes, and going back to work.

Americans were eager to forget the war now: they wanted to return to the lives they had lived before the conflict began. When, in 1921, Warren G. Harding succeeded Wilson to the presidency, he said he would return the country to what he called "normalcy."

The normalcy which everyone seemed to want meant different things to different groups of people. To the big industrialists it meant freedom to conduct their plants as they wished without the restraints they had submitted to in wartime; it meant making what arrangements they wished with respect to wages and hours of work.

But labor also was anxious to get back to prewar conditions. The cost of living had now reached twice what it had been before the war, and though labor had agreed patriotically not to strike in wartime, the war was over now. The workers saw no reason why they should not strike if that was necessary to get better wages.

It was natural enough for people to want to throw off the restrictions that had bound them in wartime. But no one can return to times that are past. Carl Sandburg, the poet, has pointed out that time brings changes even "into a world resenting change." Changes came to America now not only because of happenings within her own borders, but because of events in far-off Russia.

In 1917 the people of Russia had killed the Czar, together with his wife and children. And after a period of terror and anxiety the communist regime established itself there.

The American people knew very little about the new Russian government. It was said that private buying and selling were prohibited under it and that cash wages were no longer paid at all. Instead of pay, workers were given cards for food, clothing, and other necessities, while the government provided them with free lodging and transportation. Those who did not work received nothing at all, it was rumored: even their vote was taken away from them.

It was said, moreover, that the peasants were in as much difficulty as were the city people: the government took all their crops and left them only just enough to feed their families. Perhaps most startling of all was the report that money in the new regime was practically valueless. There were no private banks, no checking accounts, no opportunity for saving, or for making loans.

Such hard conditions did apparently prevail while the Russians were adjusting themselves to their new government. The rumors of them terrified the American people. What if communism came to the United States? they asked. Suppose the United States abandoned her old ways and took up these radical new doctrines? Were the Communists actually working to establish themselves in America? Were they actually trying now to overturn the government that had been established by Washington and Jefferson?

A wave of hysteria swept across the country. If Communists were working in America in their insidious ways, they must be got rid of. Every organization that was at all radical in its point of view was suspect—and especially every labor organization. The foreign-born were feared most of all. Every strike at that time was said to be communist-inspired.

Gompers and the American Federation of Labor had proven themselves loyal, conservative Americans during the war, but people suspected even them now. Everywhere workingmen were looked on with suspicion. What right had they to be prosperous? people were asking. They wear silk shirts, it was reported in derision. They buy their wives silk stockings. People were nervous and fearful.

So whenever a strike did occur it was felt that Communists had caused it. It was not necessary to have any evidence to prove this—people had made up their minds in advance that all labor difficulties were caused by the Communists.

In 1919, sixty thousand men in Seattle, Washington, went out on a general strike. The strike was broken by the state and local governments. Everyone was sure the Communists had stirred up the trouble.

And when in that same year there was a strike of the Boston police, the people were frightened and enraged, and the strike was put down by the state militia.

The Seattle and Boston strikes were comparatively small affairs. The great steel strike of 1919 was nationwide. The workers in the steel mills were almost all of foreign origin. They were Poles, Serbs, Italians, and some Negroes. The Negroes were the only ones who spoke English well. These men worked in the steel mills generally for twelve hours a day, and for six days a week. They lived in primitive shacks, and their wages were low.

There had been unsuccessful attempts to organize the steelworkers in 1902 and again in 1910. But in 1919 William Z. Foster, a radical who had been a member of the I. W. W., started to go around among the workers telling them that if they would organize they could have better working conditions. The workers listened to him. Those who did not understand English had what he said translated for them. In a short time a hundred thousand men in Pittsburgh and the other steel cities had agreed to join the union.

Now representatives of the newly formed union went to see Elbert Gary, who was chairman of the United States Steel Corporation, and asked that he make a trade agreement with them. "Our corporation and subsidiaries, although they do not combat labor unions as such, decline to discuss business with them," Gary said.

So the steelworkers walked out of the mills and the strike began. The men asked for collective bargaining, an eight-hour day, and better wages.

The United States Steel Corporation was the richest industry in the United States and indeed in the world. It had plenty of money to hire strikebreakers and it brought them to Pittsburgh and the other steel cities by the thousands. It employed two well-known detective agencies to plant labor spies among the strikers, and instructed them to stir up racial animosities between Negroes and white men, and between Italians and Serbs. It used local police and state militia to break up picket lines and union meetings. It placed full-page advertisements in the leading newspapers to persuade the public that the strike was communist-inspired.

The steel companies talked so much of communist influence among the workmen that most of the public were persuaded that the whole strike had been negotiated by the Russians. Was not William Z. Foster himself a radical? The steelworkers were foreigners anyway— they were "hunkies," "dagoes," and "wops."

So strong was the tide of feeling against the steelworkers that certain thoughtful men began to question it. A group of Protestant churchmen, the Interchurch World Movement, set up a commission of inquiry to investigate the strike. But the commission could find no evidence of foreign intrigue among the strikers. They announced that the excitement against communism was entirely baseless as far as the strike was concerned.

Nevertheless, the union members had no way of combating the growing storm that had risen against them, and their discouragement grew until finally they asked the Interchurch Commission to meet with the steel companies and mediate for them. They would accept any terms whatsoever that resulted from such mediation, they said.

But the steel companies refused to meet with the Interchurch Commission. "There is nothing to mediate," they said.

So the strike at last was broken, and the strikers drifted back to work. But the Interchurch Commission issued a final report, saying:

The United States Steel Corporation was too big to be beaten by 300,000 workingmen. It had too large a cash surplus, too many allies among other businesses, too much support from government officers, local and national, too strong influence with social institutions such as the press and the pulpit, it spread over too much of the earth—still retaining absolutely centralized control—to be defeated by widely scattered workers of many minds, many fears, varying states of pocketbooks, and under a comparatively improvised leadership.

There were other strikes that year—one of the biggest of them was in the coal mines. And every time the men left their jobs and set up their picket lines, the public was convinced that Russians were responsible. (This is the point of view of many people still.) But though there were indeed some Communists in the labor unions their influence was not great. The men were organizing into unions because individually they had no strength when they were confronted by the massed power of the great corporations. What they wanted were shorter hours, better wages, and better working conditions.

XVIII

Welfare Capitalism and the Great Depression

The government was being run by businessmen in the 1920's: it was a time of astonishing prosperity. American workingmen who had jobs were more prosperous than they had ever been—they were able to buy radios, automobiles, and well-made clothes. But despite this fact there were about a million men out of work. Ingenious new machinery was in large part responsible for their unemployment.

So there was an uneasiness beneath all the excitement and prosperity of the twenties, for new machines were being invented that were so ingenious they could work with very little help from men. And this meant the loss of jobs for many. The term "technological unemployment," meaning unemployment that resulted when machines did the work, was beginning to have a dread meaning.

Now the terror that haunted every man was not that he would fail to earn enough money to support his family, but that some day he would lose his job altogether, not because he did not work hard and well, but because a machine was doing the work that he could do. Almost every workingman was haunted by the fear that some day he would lose his job and fail to find another.

What could a man do to secure himself against unemployment? When America was first settled every workingman owned his own house and had some land around it where he could do a little gardening in his spare time. That meant that he had food and shelter, no matter what befell him. Now, however, most workmen lived in rented places, and if they could not pay the rent they were evicted. Now it was necessary to have money to pay for food, for there was no chance of raising food in a modern industrial city. The thought of unemployment was enough to keep many men awake at night.

But there was fear in the minds of the capitalists, too. They were afraid that organized labor might grow too strong, and take their power away from them. It was true that the United States Steel Corporation had crushed the steel strike, but not all the companies were as rich as United States Steel. So the big industrialists pondered on ways to prevent the unions from getting strong. They organized a great anti-union drive in the 1920's. Black lists, which held the names of those who were sympathetic to organized labor, were circulated among employers. No man whose name was on the list was given a job. Besides this, new employees were required to sign "yellow-dog contracts" in which they promised that if they were hired they would not take part in any union activities. And labor spies were placed here and there in the plants to keep the management informed about the activities of possible union sympathizers.

Racketeers were discovered in some of the unions at about this time. They were found especially in the building trades in San Francisco, Chicago, and New York. Much publicity was given to them, as if to persuade the public that all unions were corrupt.

At the very center of the anti-union drive was the movement for the open shop. An open shop is one in which both union and non-union men are employed. Members of the National Manufacturers Association, of various chambers of commerce, and of other employers' associations insisted that since the open shop meant the right of the employer to hire anyone he wished, and the right of the worker to join a union or not as he chose, the open shop was a democratic organization. But union men pointed out that no employer in an open shop would be likely to hire a union man. The open shop, they said, meant the end of collective bargaining. It distressed them to have the open shop called "The American Plan"—as if union members were not good Americans.

The talk of the American Plan and the other tactics which the employers used did not destroy organized labor. And now, once again, management began to appeal to the courts for injunctions against strikes. The Clayton Act, toward which labor had looked so hopefully, had proven ineffectual. Between 1918 and 1928 three hundred and eighty-nine injunctions were issued.

Unable to find any solution to what seemed an impasse, labor now turned to politics again. If they could elect a President who was sympathetic to them as Woodrow Wilson had been, they might get some legislation that would give them a fair chance, they thought. So they backed Senator Robert M. La Follette of Wisconsin for President. His platform was a progressive one. One plank of it read, "We favor the right of farmers and industrial workers to organize, bargain collectively through representatives of their own choosing, and conduct without hindrance cooperative enterprises."

But La Follette was soundly beaten at the polls, and

once again labor found out that the way to success was not through politics.

Meantime, in 1924, Samuel Gompers died. For many years he had been the grand old man of organized labor. He had been president of the A. F. of L. every year but one since its beginning. That one year was 1894, when John McBride was elected.

Now, at Gompers' death, all labor mourned him. And the industrialists mourned him, too, for he had truly been a conservative and had tried all his life to bridge the gap between capital and labor. Newspaper editorials questioned what kind of man would succeed him. Would radical leaders get control of labor's ranks? Would there be a split between the radical and conservative labor elements?

They need not have worried. The new president of the A. F. of L. was William Green of the United Mine Workers. The son of Welsh immigrants, he had been born in Ohio and had worked in the mine pits since he was a boy.

Green was a very sober, sedate man, with a plump figure, "a round, humorless face," a soft voice, and a quiet manner. Frances Perkins, who was Secretary of Labor under Franklin D. Roosevelt, said he was "the mildest and most polite of men." He reassured the A. F.

of L. on his installation as president by saying that it would be his "steadfast purpose to adhere to those fundamental principles of trade-unionism so amply championed by Mr. Gompers." It did not seem that the A. F. of L. would be much more dangerous under Green's leadership than it had been under Gompers'.

Still the employers did not like organized labor any more than they ever had. They soon discovered a new way to combat it. This new idea was "Welfare Capitalism."

Under the system of Welfare Capitalism, an effort was made to have the employees of each company feel that they were members of "One Big Family"—that the interests of the company and the interests of the workingmen were one.

It was easy to prove that if each "Big Family" was to prosper, everyone must work as hard as possible and produce as much as he could. Some time earlier a so-called efficiency expert, named Frederick W. Taylor, had written a book in which he proved that time and materials were lost by using inefficient methods. He had studied each motion used in the production of an article, and as a result of this study he was able to tell each worker how he ought to stand, and move, and lift, and set things down again, so that finished products would come pouring faster and faster from the machines. Efficiency was the refrain to which all the work was now to be done.

Naturally the workers, being used to working according to their own rate and pattern, did not like Taylor's efficiency methods very much. But they were placated by being told that if they worked and produced more they would have a larger share of the profits. A regular system of profit sharing was set up, and employees were given an opportunity to buy stock in their companies so that if business was good they would have their share.

In addition to all this, the employees of a great many companies were encouraged to join unions—but these were company unions. Such unions were like any others except that representatives of management sat in at all meetings to keep track of what was going on, to advise the management of any action taken, and to advise the employees of the management's point of view.

There were also many benefits to make the employees contented under the new Welfare Capitalism plan of the twenties. Systems of retirement pensions were arranged, and there were cafeterias where employees could buy nourishing food as well as clinics where their health was looked after. Provision was made for social clubs, for glee clubs, and picnics, and baseball games with employees from rival concerns. The companies even raised wages so that they equaled or surpassed those demanded by organized labor.

All these things were done at great expense to the companies, but the management estimated that a contented working force increased efficiency in the plants concerned and cut down the "labor turnover," that is, it prevented workers from shifting from one plant to another. The expense involved in this new system was very great indeed, but it was far less than it would have been if the workers joined a regular A. F. of L. union which might have gone on strike.

Undoubtedly the workers benefited under these new plans. And the companies were successful in what they set out to do, for the numbers who joined the regular unions fell off. Usually in times of prosperity union membership increased, but now the numbers who joined A. F. of L. unions declined rapidly, and the number of strikes declined also. It looked as if the drive against organized labor had succeeded. But then in 1929 the Great Depression came. And that nearly put an end to Welfare Capitalism.

Every kind of business had to retrench when the depression struck the country: the retrenchments made were generally at the expense of the workers. Wages were cut and cut again long before dividends were cut. Then workers were discharged. Seven million people were out of work by the end of 1930: by 1932 there were fifteen million unemployed. All the profit-sharing plans, the glee clubs, the company magazines, and the bowling clubs were forgotten. The company unions could do nothing to help the misery and hunger of the unemployed. Men out of work cued up in the breadlines, and sat at the street corners wondering whether their shabby coats would hang together for another winter, or whether they could find friends to take them in when they could no longer pay the rent. They were listless and apathetic, having no plans and not knowing what to do about their plight. The failure of capitalism in the Great Depression was too baffling for them to cope with.

William Green of the A. F. of L. did have a plan, to be sure. He said that if the number of hours in the working day were cut down, there would be more work to go around and more people would be employed. But no one listened to Green's plan, or at least it was not put into effect.

And Congress, too, belatedly passed some legislation designed to help labor. The Norris-La Guardia Act of 1932 assured labor of its right to organize, forbade "yellow-dog contracts," and outlawed injunctions. But these provisions were of little use to men who had no jobs. There seemed to be nothing that anyone could do for the unemployed. And then Franklin D. Roosevelt was sent to the White House.

XIX

"Only in Free Lands—"

―――――――――――――

"A host of unemployed citizens face the grim problem of existence, and an equally great number toil with little return. Only a foolish optimist can deny the dark realities of the moment. . . . Our great primary task is to put people to work."

It was March, 1933, and Franklin Roosevelt was making his inaugural speech. A third of all the wage earners in America were unemployed that spring. Breadlines and soup kitchens had been set up in the cities everywhere. For though the guns were quiet again, and the soldiers had come home, America had not been able to recover from the war. There had been a boom in the twenties but it was short-lived. Coal mining, shipbuilding, textile manufacturing, the making of railroad equipment—none of these industries had permanently come back to the prewar level of production. Farmers could not find markets for what they produced. Retail shops had shut down by the thousands, having no customers. One after another the banks were closing. Economic depression such as this had never occurred before in all of America's history. Nevertheless, the voice of the new President was reassuring. "There is nothing to fear," he said, and his words coming over the radio were listened to eagerly in every part of the country. "There is nothing to fear, but fear itself."

The depression of the early thirties was no sudden thing. Evidences of it had been appearing gradually for a long time. Herbert Hoover's administration, however, believed in "rugged individualism" and said that every man who really wanted it could find a job.

Two chickens in every pot, two automobiles in every garage—if people would only purchase more, prosperity would return. Prosperity was just around the corner, anyway.

But most people in Hoover's time had no money with which to buy luxuries. Many had none to buy food. A group of unemployed marched to Washington to explain their plight to Hoover, but they were driven away. On the street corners in many cities men sat at little stands selling apples to earn what they could, while others stopped the passers-by for a dime with which they could buy coffee or something to eat.

Hoover did, however, take some measures to alleviate the business depression. He created the Reconstruction Finance Corporation to save the railroads, banks, and some industries from collapse by giving them loans. Prosperity at the top, he thought, would trickle down to the workers at the bottom.

The Reconstruction Finance Corporation may indeed have done some good, but the trickle of prosperity was too slow to reach the great masses of the unemployed. In 1932 fifteen million men were unemployed. With their families they made up a quarter of the population of the country.

Franklin D. Roosevelt was more realistic in his approach to the problems that beset the country. America's economy must somehow be brought into balance or the whole structure would collapse.

"What we seek is balance in our economic system," Roosevelt said. "Balance between agriculture and industry, and balance between the wage earner, the employer, and the consumer. We seek also balance that our internal markets be kept rich and large, and that our trade with other nations be increased on both sides of the ledger."

Roosevelt knew, however, that these fine balances could never be attained while there were millions of men out of work. Unemployment was the first problem to be attacked. And every day that problem was growing to greater proportions.

Roosevelt did not believe that the best way to help the unemployed was by giving them money; he thought very little of the "dole." People kept their self-respect if they worked for wages, he maintained. And since industry could not provide work for all who wanted it, he proposed that the government should do so. He persuaded the Congress to appropriate large sums of money which were to be used in vast useful projects. The projects, when completed, would benefit the country as a whole, the spending of money would "prime the pump" and help get industry going again, and those who had been without work would be usefully employed.

Various great projects were soon under way. The first of them was started only about two months after Roosevelt took office. It was the Civilian Conservation Corps. The CCC, as it was called, provided employment for the boys who had finished school but who could find no work to do. Now they were put to work in a grand program to conserve America's natural resources. It might be said that they themselves were one of America's greatest resources which were now to be saved by working for others.

Soon, therefore, in every part of the country CCC camps were built to house the 300,000 boys who for the first time were to be gainfully employed, and the boys were leaving the crowded cities and boarding the trains that would take them to a new life of work.

Those boys fought forest fires, and sprayed insect pests; they dug irrigation ditches and worked on soil conservation; they chopped out fire lanes in the forests; and planted thousands of young trees on federal and state lands. The work of the CCC continued for nearly ten years, and America was infinitely richer because of it.

Meantime another and much larger undertaking was started. This was the Works Progress Administration which was generally known as the WPA. Under the program huge amounts of money were appropriated for public works. Post offices, hospitals, schools, libraries, and courthouses were soon under construction in every part of the country. Those who planned, designed, and built them were the former unemployed. They also built new roads, new bridges, dams, and power stations. There were others besides the manual workers who had been caught in the Great Depression. There were teachers, writers, artists, actors, and musicians. Programs to use their talents were started also. They played in concerts in the public parks and painted murals on the walls of post offices; they undertook great projects of historical research and published detailed guides to every state. Where there had been idleness and despair, now there was activity and hope.

Many criticized the work of the WPA; there were jokes about men resting on their shovels. And many were horrified at the enormous amount of money that was being spent. Congress appropriated almost eleven billion dollars for the WPA. But when all was said and done, the fact remained that millions of men and women who had been miserable and idle were back at work again.

Good as all this was, however, the country needed more than simply work for the unemployed. It needed to get the complicated machinery of production going again.

"Lock yourselves in a room and stay there until you have made a plan," Roosevelt is said to have told his advisers.

The plan that was worked out in this way was embodied in the National Industrial Recovery Act, or NIRA, which was passed by Congress and signed by the President in June, 1933. The administrator of the new plan was General Hugh Johnson. Its symbol was the Blue Eagle.

Some radical elements in the country had urged that the government take over the industries to run them itself, but this was not done. Instead, each industry was permitted to make its own code of production and profits. The industrialists were given complete freedom to work in their own way, but the rights of the workers were safeguarded under Section 7 (a)—a section which was to become famous. This stipulated that all employees should have the right to organize and bargain collectively. It provided, moreover, that no one should be required to join a company union and that employers must agree to certain standards with regard to workers' hours and pay.

The NIRA was hailed joyfully by nearly everyone at first. There were great parades in which the men of various industries carried signs and banners bearing Blue Eagles. Here was a chance to get back to the old prewar ways, the industrialists thought. And labor rejoiced in the belief that it could organize again.

But the NIRA did not work. There were arguments and dissensions. In less than two years the whole thing fell apart. When in May, 1935, the Supreme Court declared that the act was unconstitutional, no one regretted it very much.

The failure of NIRA brought disillusionment and

discouragement to all those who had been so enthusiastic. But one part of the plan was salvaged. This was Section 7 (a). Only eleven days before the Court handed down its decision the Wagner Act was passed. And the Wagner Act embodied the same labor provisions NIRA had had.

The Wagner Act, which was officially called the National Labor Relations Act, was definitely and clearly pro-labor in its point of view. It gave organized labor a position which it had never had before. Franklin Roosevelt said of it, "By preventing practices which tend to destroy the independence of labor, it seeks for every worker within its scope, that freedom of choice and action which is justly his."

How did it give every worker that freedom? Under the new act the employer was forbidden in any way to interfere with labor's activity in organizing. He was forbidden to restrain his employees from joining whatever union they wished, and he was required to bargain with them collectively. He was forbidden to dominate or control any union or even to contribute to it. This, of course, meant the outlawing of company unions though some of them were later to be revived.

Because it was not at all easy to see that the provisions of the new act were obeyed, a special board was set up to enforce it. This was the National Labor Relations Board. Its three members supervised union elections to see that they were carried on without interference. They also heard complaints and arbitrated disputes.

The Wagner Act appeared to sweep away the restraints under which organized labor had worked so long and, on the whole, it had the support of the public.

But the industrialists were enraged by it. Surely it was unconstitutional, they said. They did not hesitate to flout its provisions since they were sure it would soon be swept from the books.

Now that organized labor was beginning to feel more secure, and the employers more intransigent, strike after strike broke out. There were strikes in the steel mills, in the automobile and rubber industries, and in the textile mills. Particularly in the great mass-production industries there was strike after strike. And now the courts were called on to issue scores of injunctions. The industrialists were so sure the new law would soon be abolished that they behaved as if it had never been written.

As matters went thus from bad to worse, a committee of the Senate was set up to investigate. Its chairman was Robert M. La Follette of Wisconsin.

The committee's investigation brought out some very

startling facts. They found that 2,500 different corporations had hired labor spies and planted them in their factories. The Burns and Pinkerton detective agencies alone had supplied 3,871 men. These detectives had managed to join the unions, and many of them had succeeded in becoming union officials. One automobile corporation had spent $830,000 for spies, strikebreakers, and munitions. Perhaps the committee's most striking figures were brought to light when they investigated the Little Steel Strike and discovered that the Youngstown Sheet and Tube Company had on hand before the strike:

> 8 machine guns
> 369 rifles
> 190 shotguns
> 450 revolvers
> 6,000 rounds of ball ammunition
> 109 gas guns
> 3,000 rounds of gas ammunition

"That would be adequate munitions for a small war," Senator La Follette said.

Despite the fact that industry was sure the Wagner Act would be abolished, it remained. On April 12, 1937, the Supreme Court handed down the decision that the

Wagner Act was constitutional. Chief Justice Charles Evans Hughes in his opinion wrote:

Employees have as clear a right to organize and select their representatives for lawful purposes, as the respondent had to organize its business and select its own officers and agents. Discrimination and coercion to prevent the free exercise of the right of employees to self-organization and representation is a proper subject for condemnation by competent legislative authority.

Long ago we stated the reason for labor organizations. We said that they were organized out of the necessities of the situation; that a single employee was helpless in dealing with an employer; that he was dependent ordinarily on his daily wage for the maintenance of himself and his family; that if the employer refused to pay him the wages he thought fair, he was nevertheless unable to leave the employ and resist arbitrary and unfair treatment; that union was essential to give laborers opportunity to deal on an equality with their employer. . . .

Meantime other measures that improved labor's fortunes had been put into effect. Among these was the Social Security Act, which was passed in August, 1935. Roosevelt said he considered it the "cornerstone of his administration." The European countries had provided social security for their workers long before this: America was the last great industrial country to see the need of it.

The Social Security Act provided that unemployment insurance should be handled by the separate states, but old-age pensions were to be administered by the federal government with funds paid in by both employer and employee. The act provided also that the federal government should give assistance to the states for the care of the blind, crippled, and disabled, and for dependent children.

With all these many diverse ideas taking concrete form as the years of the early thirties passed, there were still three problems that had not been solved, although the labor unions had been seeking solutions for them for many years. They were the questions of child labor, of the standardization of maximum hours of work and minimum rates of pay. In May, 1938, in a talk to the people over the radio, President Roosevelt said:

"A self-supporting and self-respecting democracy can plead no justification for the existence of child labor, no economic reason for chiseling workers' wages or stretching workers' hours."

The Fair Labor Standards bill became law in June, 1938. It established a minimum wage of twenty-five cents an hour, and a forty-four-hour week, and prohibited the employment of children under sixteen in industries whose products entered interstate commerce.

The provisions for wages and hours were moderate at the beginning, but they were to be raised as time went on.

The legislation of the Roosevelt administration had in truth brought a "new deal" to labor. Conditions which labor had fought for many years to attain had now come to pass. The courts were no longer hostile to labor's aims as they had been in the past. Labor's right to organize was now an accepted fact. There was a triumphant note in Roosevelt's voice when he said, addressing a labor convention:

"Only in free lands have free labor unions survived. When union workers assemble with freedom and independence in a convention like this, it is a proof the American democracy has remained unimpaired; it is a symbol of our determination to keep it free."

XX

John L. Lewis and the C. I. O.

John L. Lewis of the United Mine Workers sat at the convention of the A. F. of L. in San Francisco in 1934, and scowled. His bushy eyebrows were more prominent than his blue eyes, his jutting jaw more prominent than any other feature of his rather rugged face. He weighed 225 pounds.

Lewis was a well-known figure at labor meetings. Much was later to be said and written of him. It was to be said that he was a consummate actor, and a dedicated leader; that he had defiant courage; that he was pompous; that he was an opportunist; and that he was a patriot. When all this has been considered, it must be acknowledged that he did a great deal to help the coal miners.

Lewis had been born in 1880, the son of a Welsh coal miner who had come to this country five years before. He had gone to work in the pits when he was twelve, and when he was still quite young had worked at organizing the miners. Soon he was acting as field representative for the A. F. of L., and he was first vice-president of the United Mine Workers and then president. He understood the dangers of the mines, the dirt, the poor pay, the bad housing—he understood all these things, for he was a miner himself. In 1919 when the country was at war, the miners had again struck against the mine owners, and the government had taken over the mines. The A. F. of L. had said this was an "outrageous proceeding," but Lewis had backed the government. "The miners cannot strike against their own government," he said. He was forty then, and his patriotic stand had cost him some popularity among the miners, but his influence was soon restored again. He had enormous popularity with them.

William Green, who presided at the meeting of the convention of the A. F. of L. in San Francisco, was a very different man. He, too, was a miner and the son of a Welsh miner. He, too, had come up through various minor offices of the A. F. of L., and had been appointed by Gompers as one of the vice-presidents. Lewis himself had helped in Green's progress. His climb to the presidency of the A. F. of L. had been steady and uneventful. Green was a sedate and dignified man. He had taught

Sunday school and his friends said that he neither drank nor smoked.

So at the San Francisco convention of 1934 John L. Lewis sat and scowled at Green, and Green, presiding, tried to ignore Lewis, for there was a deep disagreement between them. Green believed that none but skilled craftsmen should be members of the A. F. of L. The painters, carpenters, electricians, bricklayers, garment workers—all these and others who were skilled in their crafts were the ones who should be organized, he thought. Any who were likely to pull down the work standards and therefore the wage rates should be kept out of the unions. There was not room in the A. F. of L. for unskilled foreigners, for Negroes, or for women. The unions he believed in were craft unions. Lewis, on the other hand, saw no reason why the unskilled should not be organized. They probably needed organization more than the others, he argued. The miners and the steelworkers were already organized but the automobile plants had no unions: they had assembly lines where men stood putting a certain bolt on a certain part of a chassis until the monotony of the task exhausted them. From time to time the moving belt that carried the chassis was speeded up so that they had to work faster and faster. The men dreaded this "speed-up." Ought not these men to be organized, so that they could try to shorten their monotonous hours of work, and protest against the speed-up?

It was easy to see, moreover, that the new methods of mass production were doing away with skilled crafts anyway. Anyone could learn to do the work that the mass-production industries required. The old days of apprentices, journeymen, and skilled craftsmen were gone forever. Since there were no longer craftsmen to any great extent, there was not much need of craft unions.

Lewis and his followers therefore believed that unions should not be organized according to crafts, but that all the workers in a given industry should be brought together in a single union. In the automobile industry, for example, metalworkers, engineers, painters, night watchmen, maintenance men, and bookkeepers—all the skilled and all the unskilled—should be brought together into a single union, an industrial union.

When Lewis proposed his plans at the A. F. of L. meeting there was bitter opposition. The arguments continued for several days, and the big coal miner apparently gloried in them. "They are striking at me hip and thigh ... right merrily shall I return their blows," he said.

William Green and the A. F. of L. were conservative.

They did not want to change their old ways, but they wanted peace in the ranks. Perhaps the agitation would die down.

But it did not die down. In 1935 the A. F. of L. convention was held in Atlantic City. And Lewis with his set jaw and beetling brow was there again. And soon he had become so enraged that he bore down on William L. Hutcheson of the Carpenters Union and dealt him a blow on the jaw with the full weight of his 225 pounds. The two men were pulled apart before more harm could be done.

Lewis now was thoroughly exasperated at what he regarded as the slowness and inaction of the A. F. of L., at their unwillingness to accept new ideas. "The A. F. of L. unions are dying off like grass under an autumn sun," he said. New vigor, new ideas were needed.

When it appeared that the advocates of industrial unionism could not be brushed aside, the A. F. of L. officials decided to try to placate them. They appointed a committee called the Committee for Industrial Organization, to study the situation and report back. The committee was to work within the framework of the A. F. of L., and its efforts were to be "educational and advisory."

But the bitterness between Green and Lewis continued. Lewis resigned from the A. F. of L. "Dear Sir and Brother," he wrote to Green, "Effective this date, I resign as vice-president of the American Federation of Labor."

While these things were going on Lewis and his followers were working hard at organizing industrial unions in the mass-production industries, and the A. F. of L. officials were becoming more and more enraged. Green pleaded with Lewis to give up his activities, and Lewis laughed at him. "I fear his threats as much as I believe his promises," Lewis said.

So the angry controversy raged, and in 1937 ten unions that had been represented on the Committee for Industrial Organization were expelled from the A. F. of L. Only the International Ladies' Garment Workers was allowed to remain.

Then in May, 1938, the committee transformed itself into the Permanent Congress of Industrial Organizations. The C. I. O. had come into being.

Under the skilled new leadership of the C. I. O., unions in the steel, radio, automobile, rubber, and many other industries were organized. In steel, where the memories of the Homestead Strike of 1892 and the steel strike of 1919 were still bitter, union members multiplied from day to day, and John L. Lewis proclaimed over the radio: "Let him who will, be he economic tyrant or sordid mercenary, pit his strength against this mighty upsurge of human sentiment now being crystallized in the hearts of thirty million workers who clamor for the establishment of industrial democracy and for participation in its tangible fruits. He is a madman or a fool who believes that this river of human sentiment . . . can be dammed or impounded by the erection of temporary barriers of restraint."

Under the vigorous leadership of the C. I. O. membership in the unions of the mass-production industries grew by leaps and bounds. The steelworkers union soon had 100,000 members, and in 1937 Myron C. Taylor, chairman of the board of the United States Steel Corporation, was ready to negotiate with their representative. No threat of strike had been necessary: the very size of the union had made U. S. Steel ready to come to terms.

Tom Girdler, who was the anti-labor president of the Republic Steel Company, did not comply so easily. The workers in his plants struck, and the strike was not broken until ten of them lay dead in the street in what has been called the Memorial Day Massacre. That was in South Chicago, May 30, 1937. They were killed in violence attending the struggle for union recognition. The C. I. O. had met its first defeat.

In the automobile industry the work of the C. I. O. was as aggressive as it had been in steel. Wages in that industry were still under $1,000 a year, and the speed-up on the assembly line was exhausting the men, while labor spies were doing their work at every corner of the great factories. "We don't want to be driven; we don't want to be spied on," the workers kept repeating.

The strike of the automobile workers began in the Fisher Body Plant in Flint, Michigan. Later it spread to Detroit, Cleveland, and Toledo. At Flint, workers did not leave the factories, they simply sat down on their work benches and refused to leave the plants. Under the leadership of Homer Martin, a quiet, bespectacled man who had formerly been a Baptist minister, they continued to sit there day after day. Food was brought in to them through the picket lines, and there was no violence and no damage to company property. It was January, and the company turned off all heat in the factories, but still the men sat it out. The company appealed to Governor Murphy of Michigan to use the state militia to force the men out of the factory, but he refused to do so, fearing what the strikers called "a blood bath."

While the "sit-down" was going on, John L. Lewis was attempting unsuccessfully to negotiate with William S. Knudsen, vice-president of General Motors Corporation. After a week in which no agreement could be reached, Franklin D. Roosevelt used his influence to effect a settlement, and the sit-down was called off.

The idea of the sit-down strike spread quickly to other industries, however. Rubber, glass, and textile workers refused to leave their shops; five-and-ten-cent store clerks sat behind their counters and refused to sell; pie bakers, opticians, dressmakers, and apartment-house janitors—all tried the sit-down strike.

The sit-down strike was declared illegal when it was brought to court. It was held that the workers were trespassing on their employers' property. But before this decision was made the public had grown resentful of sit-down strikes and the inconvenience they were causing.

The C. I. O. was blamed for the unpopular sit-down strikes. People said that the new organization was radical and aggressive, and that it had stirred up trouble unnecessarily. They even said that the C. I. O. wanted to upset the government: that it was communist-controlled.

It was true, of course, that the C. I. O. was much more aggressive than the old A. F. of L. had been. It was even true that there were Communists in some of the C. I. O. unions. But those unions were not communist-controlled, and they did not want to upset the United States government. Their aims, indeed, were almost exactly the same as those of the A. F. of L.: they wanted fairer working conditions, better pay, shorter hours for those who worked. The great difference between them and the older unions lay in the fact that they wanted these things for *all* the people who worked, not for just a chosen few. They wanted them for the women who were entering industry in larger and larger numbers, for the Negroes who were coming up from the South to compete with the northern workingmen in the factories, for the foreign-born.

There was another difference between the C. I. O. and the A. F. of L.—the C. I. O. was much more eager to take part in politics. The new unions were not nearly so rich as the old A. F. of L. unions had been. They could not do so much for their members in the way of unemployment, sickness, or death benefits. Therefore, they looked to the government for social legislation.

In the belief that his administration would further such legislation, John L. Lewis and the C. I. O. backed Franklin D. Roosevelt for re-election in 1936. But after Roosevelt's election Lewis grew more and more ambitious and eager for power. It has been said that he sought the vice-presidency of the United States and offered to use his influence in the C. I. O. to back Roosevelt's re-election in 1940.

Whether this is true or not, he fell out with Roosevelt. On October 25, 1940, he broadcast an amazing speech to the C. I. O. members. In it he said:

I think the re-election of President Roosevelt for a third term would be a national evil of the first magnitude. He no longer hears the cries of the people. . . .

It is obvious that President Roosevelt will not be re-elected for a third term unless he has the overwhelming support of the men and women of labor. If he is, therefore, it will mean that the members of the Congress of Industrial Organizations have rejected my advice and recommendations. I will accept the result as being equivalent of a vote of no confidence and will retire as president of the Congress of Industrial Organizations in November.

When Roosevelt was re-elected after that, John L. Lewis kept his word. He resigned as president of the C. I. O., and Philip Murray, a quiet, soft-spoken man who had been vice-president of the United Mine Workers, was elected to take his place. Murray was to hold that post until he died of a heart attack in 1952.

XXI

"We Feel Confident—"

On the morning of August 14, 1945, all the whistles in America were blowing, for the last bomb had fallen and the last shot had been fired: World War II was over, and the soldiers were coming home. Crowded on the decks of the vessels soon after that, the young veterans looked toward the land and wondered what was in store for them.

Those who had been working for America at home wondered, too. In factories, mills, and mines the no-strike pledge for the duration of the war had been made and generally kept. Government regulation had made wages high, and the workers, cooperating with management and with the government, had done an extraordinary job of production.

Between June, 1940, and July, 1945, according to Foster Rhea Dulles in *Labor in America*, they had turned out 200,000 combat planes, 71,000 naval ships, 5,000

161

cargo ships, 9,000 pieces of heavy artillery, almost 2,000,-000 heavy machine guns, 12,000,000 rifles and carbines, 86,000 tanks, 16,000 armored cars, 2,400,000 army trucks, almost 6,000,000 aircraft bombs, 537,000 depth charges. . . . The production of coal rose to the record total of more than 600,000 tons a year; electric energy output increased from 130,000 million to 230,000 million kilowatt hours, and the fabrication of steel ingots mounted from 47,000,000 to 80,000,000 tons.

But though labor's part in war production had been so spectacular, and though it was greatly praised by General Eisenhower and others, there was a feeling of uneasiness in the country. Workingmen remembered the strikes and violence that had followed World War I, and they remembered the depression. Had they come back to unemployment, to selling apples at street corners perhaps? The workers were not the only ones who were uneasy and afraid. The general public were questioning the future, too. Hadn't the unions grown too big and too powerful? they wondered. Was it good for any single group to be as strong as this? The feeling against organized labor in America was increasing every day.

A great many factories were shut down when the war was over. They were "retooling"—making over their machinery so that they could turn out peacetime products. When those factories reopened, would the thousands of returning men be able to find work? the people asked.

But there was no great unemployment problem after World War II. Fifty-five million men were soon re-employed. Through careful planning by the government many of the returning soldiers and sailors were able to continue with their education until places in industry were found for them.

The problem this time was a different one—would the wages that had been agreed to in wartime be continued in time of peace? For wage and price controls were being removed now. And since industry was making high profits, labor saw no reason why it should not share in the general prosperity. Walter Reuther, the serious-minded head of the United Automobile Workers Union, explained labor's feeling when he said, "The kind of labor movement we want is not committed to a nickel-in-the-pay-envelope department. We are building a labor movement, not to patch up the old world so men can starve less often and less frequently, but a labor movement that will remake the world so that the working people will get the benefit of their labor."

"We cannot pay more wages, unless we increase the price of manufactured articles," the industrialists said.

"Open your books to us, and let us see that you are not making enough to pay more wages," the workers retorted. But the industrialists refused.

So there were strikes again. Not strikes of violence this time as there had been in the 1890's and in the early days of the twentieth century, but long-drawn-out strikes that cost both the industrialists and the unions thousands of dollars. The unions had such large memberships now that their dues made them very rich. They could afford to hold out against the employers for months together.

There were strikes in the automobile industry, and in steel; the railway trainmen struck, and so did the airplane pilots, and the seamen and longshoremen; while Lewis called the eighth strike in five years in the coal mines.

Meantime living costs were steadily increasing. To meet the rising cost of living the unions asked for a wage increase of 23 per cent, pointing to the fact that corporate profits had risen 50 per cent. When their demands were refused, the unions called for more strikes. This situation was bad enough for both management and labor but they were not the only ones concerned in these strikes: the public was also involved. And the public was impatient. People disliked being hindered from traveling on railroads or airplanes. They were worried when the coal supply was cut off in the winter. And all the time the cost of living was rising and rising, and they had to find someone to blame for this. If organized labor did not demand such high wages, prices would not be so high, people said.

In 1945 the popular feeling against organized labor was reflected in Congress where a Republican majority had been elected. Congress was determined that legislation must be passed which would control and curb the great power of the labor unions. Labor must be made to show a greater sense of responsibility to the people, it was said. Once the Sherman Anti-Trust Act had been passed to curb the vast power of the trusts. Now it was the labor unions that must be controlled. They had grown too big and too powerful. That, at least, was the drift of the popular talk.

This was why the Taft-Hartley bill was made law. President Truman vetoed it. He said it was "shocking— bad for labor, bad for management, bad for the country." But the bill was passed anyway, over the President's veto.

The Taft-Hartley Law is a very complicated act which contains scores of provisions. These provisions, while they do not deny the rights which were granted

165

to labor in the Wagner Act, add a long list intended to safeguard the rights of the employers. Among the many provisions of the bill is one that expressly bans the closed shop, and another that provides that where there is a union contract, a strike may not be called without sixty days' notice. The act also provides that unions may be sued in court for breach of contract; that unions are forbidden to make contributions to political campaigns; and that union officials must make an affidavit swearing that they do not belong to the Communist party.

There were many other provisions in the long Taft-Hartley Act, and labor, reading them, maintained that Congress was trying to destroy organized labor. Whether this was the case or not, the emphasis of the bill was very different from that of the Wagner Act.

Labor protested vigorously against the Taft-Hartley Act. They said it must be repealed. If it was not repealed, it must at least be modified. Agitation over the new measure colored the platforms of both Republicans and Democrats in the succeeding elections. Both parties promised to modify the bill—but, as time passed, neither did anything about it. The Taft-Hartley Act, which some labor men now called the "slave labor act," remained in effect unchanged.

But though organized labor felt that it had been dealt a severe blow by the passage of the Taft-Hartley Act, it had not been destroyed. Instead, the unions continued to grow in strength, in maturity, and in a sense of responsibility.

There had been disagreement between the A. F. of L. and the C. I. O. as to how the unions should be organized. Should there be craft unions or industrial unions? Sometimes this disagreement was so strong and the desire of each organization to gain new members so intense, that they raided each other's union lists and even called strikes against each other—"jurisdictional strikes." Now, however, both the C. I. O. and the A. F. of L. began to see that no one type of union was suitable for all industries, that craft unions were better in some industries and industrial unions in others. They admitted both.

In other ways also the A. F. of L. and the C. I. O. began to influence each other. The old A. F. of L. had been traditionally prejudiced against Negroes and the foreign-born, and had not wanted women admitted to the unions. Now, under the influence of the C. I. O., they were more liberal toward all these groups.

And while these changes were coming to the A. F. of L. the C. I. O. also was changing. The fact had been admitted for some time that there were Communists in the C. I. O. unions, although their union leadership was democratic. Now, however, the C. I. O. took a clear-cut stand against communism, and Communists were expelled from all their unions.

The A. F. of L. and the C. I. O. were drawing closer and closer together all the time. But in 1952, in the month of November, events occurred which made the two organizations more united still.

On November 9, 1952, Philip Murray, who had been president of the C. I. O. ever since John L. Lewis resigned, died suddenly of a heart attack. Twelve days later, with equal suddenness, William Green died: he had been president of the A. F. of L. for nearly thirty years.

Elections for new presidents were held in both organizations. And Walter Reuther, the dynamic leader of the United Automobile Workers, was elected president of the C. I. O., while George Meany, who had started his career as an apprentice plumber and who had held many responsible posts in the labor movement, became head of the A. F. of L. Both men were selfless, farsighted, and progressive: to both it seemed that the time had come for healing the breach between the two great organizations. To both men it was now clear that the A. F. of L.-C. I. O. should be one organization. Walter

Reuther asked that when the A. F. of L. and the C. I. O. merged into one organization, George Meany should be its president.

On February 9, 1955, announcement of the merger was made, and a joint statement, signed by both Walter Reuther and George Meany, was issued. The statement read:

We feel confident that the merger of the two union groups which we represent will be a boon to our nation and its people in this tense period. We are happy that, in our way, we have been able to bring about unity in the American labor movement. . . .

XXII

View from a Mountaintop

With the joining of the A. F. of L. and the C. I. O. the newest chapter of American labor history began. The old days of violence, of machine guns and Pinkerton detectives, were for the most part over. Now the courts were more liberal in their labor decisions. And though Taft-Hartley had curbed the power of the unions to some extent, they were stronger than they had ever been.

Organized labor was so strong now because union membership was so large. There were ten million men and women in the A. F. of L. unions, between five and six million in the C. I. O. unions, besides three million in the Railroad Brotherhoods and the independent unions. Altogether more than eighteen million Americans were carrying union cards.

These eighteen million now felt themselves a part of the great new world that was industrial America. Their part in it appeared to them exciting and full of possibilities. Walter Reuther stirred them when he said:

"This is a crusade, a crusade to gear economic abundance to human needs. We plan to take management up on the mountaintop, and we would like to give them a little bit of the vision we have. We would like to show them the great new world that can be built if free labor and free management and free government and free people can cooperate together in harnessing the power of America and gearing it to the basic needs of the people."

What was it that labor wanted to show from its mountaintop? What did labor want? Some years ago someone asked Samuel Gompers what it was that labor wanted. And Gompers had answered, "More." Didn't labor still want more?

Of course labor still wanted more. It wanted more comfort, more security, more education. But it did not want these things at the expense of America as a whole. It saw that it could not be prosperous unless the country as a whole was prosperous. Employers and employees must both be made to thrive, or neither could.

That was why David Dubinsky, president of the International Ladies' Garment Workers Union, suggested that when some of the small shops in the needle trades appeared to be on the verge of failure, the union lend them money to pull through. It would have been easy for those shops to degenerate into sweatshops with evil consequences for both employer and employee, if more capital had not been made available.

Again, when trade was falling off, with danger that many millinery establishments would have to shut down, the United Cap, Hat and Millinery Workers lent $1,000,000 to promote hat sales. So the trade was put on it's feet again and the workers kept their jobs.

The unions are so rich now that they have a responsibility to use their funds well and, with very few exceptions, they do. They have put a great deal of money into the fight against racial discrimination, and they have also appropriated funds for policing against union racketeers. In addition to this they have set aside many thousands for workers' education and for insurance benefits, since the amount workers receive from the government's social security is insufficient. The unions also have financed programs for statistical study so that they may plan for the future.

Overproduction, with resultant unemployment, was one of the most pressing problems the unions studied. When a plant made more of a commodity than it could sell, and then shut down, it threw its men temporarily out of work. This was particularly true in the automobile industry.

The Automobile Workers, therefore, employed ten economists from both Canada and the United States to study this situation. They also employed a large staff of industrial specialists. And as an outcome of all this work the idea of the "guaranteed annual wage" was evolved.

Since the Ford Company proved receptive to the idea of the guaranteed wage, it was argued that if Ford could manage to guarantee its men a regular annual wage, other industries could do so, too. So a great campaign of publicity was started to get the public to talk about the idea. There were magazine articles and radio programs, the plan was discussed on television and in club meetings. What had seemed like a visionary scheme now became quite a commonplace. It was not too much to hope that many industries would give workingmen the security they wanted.

So with imagination and vigor the unions plan for the future. They want, with the assistance of their research staff, to prove and publicize the fact that wage increases are often possible without price increases. They want to use their funds to start huge housing programs. They want to study the changes which have been brought about by new machines—to find out what to do when musicians are thrown out of work by the use of records, or linotype operators by the development of the teletype setter, or miners by the use of new mining machinery.

They want to know what happened to the second man on the bus when the Fifth Avenue Coach Company in New York City found a way to operate its busses with just one man.

Automation, the use of machines to run machines, would be more and more prevalent in the days ahead. Undoubtedly more and more men would be out of work because of it. The unions must be ready to meet this change. They must make plans.

So, in the union halls or sitting in the park on Sunday afternoon, or driving back and forth to work in their automobiles, or just standing in groups outside the door before their plants open, men and women are discussing the future and their place in it. What will this great new world be like when "free labor and free management and free government and free people . . . cooperate together in harnessing the power of America and gearing it to the needs of the people"?

Index

175

Index

Index

Index